SNAKES OF THE WORLD

Scott Weidensaul

SNAKES OF THE WORLD

Scott Weidensaul

CHARTWELL
BOOKS, INC.

A QUINTET BOOK

Published by Chartwell Books
A Division of Book Sales, Inc.
110 Enterprise Avenue
Secaucus, New Jersey 07094

This edition produced for sale in North America, its
territories and dependencies only.

ISBN 1-55521-733-8

This book was designed and produced by
Quintet Publishing Limited
6 Blundell Street
London N7 9BH

Creative Director: Terry Jeavons
Designer: Chris Dymond
Project Editors: Damian Thompson, Caroline Beattie
Editor: Rosemary Booton
Illustrator: Danny McBride

Typeset in Great Britain by
Central Southern Typesetters, Eastbourne
Manufactured in Hong Kong by
Excel Graphic Arts Company
Printed in Singapore by
Star Standard Industries Pte. Ltd.

WARNING

The publishers would like to point out that
several species covered in this book produce
venom that is toxic and therefore potentially
dangerous to human beings. All snakes should
be treated with caution.

CONTENTS

◆◆◆◆◆◆◆◆◆◆◆◆◆◆◆

INTRODUCTION

◆◆◆◆◆◆◆◆◆◆◆◆◆◆

When I was a boy, I found a small ring-neck snake under a rock in the woods behind my house, on a mild, early summer day. It was a marvellous creature, only as thick as a piece of twine and less than a foot long, glossy black on its back, orange on its belly, with a thin band of gold around its neck. I took it home and put it in an empty fish tank on my dressing-table, then went to get my friends. When I returned to show off my catch, it was gone. I hadn't realized that the snake could crawl up the corner of the lidless tank and get away. We tore the room apart looking for it, but the snake had vanished.

I looked off and on for the next few days, then quickly forgot about it, as ten-year-olds will do. (I am not sure my family forgot as quickly, since the thought of a snake loose in the house gives most people the creeps.) A few weeks later, I found a graphic reminder of my lost pet – a shed skin beneath my desk, feather-weight and grey, with a pale ring around its neck. The snake was not only still around, it was obviously thriving and growing.

I know now that the ring-neck snake was probably living in my toy-filled wardrobe, hunting for tiny spiders behind the radiator, and catching moths trapped inside the window screens. Over the next two months I found another shed skin and secretly hoarded my prizes.

Just before the summer ended, I woke one morning to find the snake curled in a patch of sunlight in the middle of the floor. It looked just as shiny as when I'd first caught it, and perhaps even a bit longer. I scooped it up and ran outside, barefoot through the dewy grass, and released it near the edge of the woods.

I still have one of the moulted skins from that snake, tucked between the dog-eared pages of a field guide to the snakes that I begged my parents to buy me not long afterwards. Over the years there would be many others, caught or simply watched, but that wayward ring-neck snake was my first real introduction to the fascinating world of serpents, where leglessness is not the handicap it might at first seem.

LEFT
Many snakes will tolerate a slow, cautious approach, for photographs or simple observation.

FACING PAGE
Harmless species like gopher snakes, rat snakes, hognoses and garter snakes make ideal pets, and are an excellent way to introduce children to snakes.

CLASSIFICATION

◆◆◆◆◆◆◆◆◆◆◆◆◆◆

Carolus Linnaeus, the eighteenth-century Swedish naturalist, counts as history's greatest 'pigeonholer'. He created the system of classification that bears his name and through which every living thing on Earth is ascribed its place in relation to all others. He quite literally created order from chaos.

The Linnean system seems complicated to the layman, but it is really quite simple. There are nine major levels, from most general to most specific; animals and plants are grouped with those sharing similar characteristics. The system uses Greek and Latin (or 'latinized' words) primarily because these languages are dead and unchanging.

For a timber rattlesnake, the classification would go like this:

RIGHT
The timber rattlesnake's scientific name *(Crotalus horridus)* is based on a system of classification that assigns each living thing to a hierarchy of relationships.

TIMBER RATTLESNAKE

Classification level	Name	Description
Kingdom	Animalia	all animals
Phylum	Chordata	all animals with notochords
Subphylum	Vertebrata	all animals with notochords encased in backbones
Class	Reptilia	cold-blooded animals with scales, and which lay eggs with leathery shells
Order	Squamata	all snakes and lizards
Family	Viperidae	vipers and pit vipers
Subfamily	Crotalinae	pit vipers
Genus	Crotalus	rattlesnakes
Species	horridus	timber rattlesnake

The combination of genus and specific name is unique for each species; the timber rattlesnake is *Crotalus horridus*, a name by which it is recognized no matter what language the scientist speaks. Many times, the same species varies from area to area — not enough to warrant classification as a separate species, but different enough to merit distinction. This is known as a sub-species, like the canebrake rattlesnake, a type of timber rattler found in the south-east of the United States. It is *Crotalus horridus atricaudatus;* sub-species names may also be written by abbreviating the first two words; *C. h. atricaudatus.* Latin names are always italicized.

Classification has traditionally been based on physical characteristics, on the assumption that closely related groups would show similar body features. Thus, the snakes were broken into about ten families — the exact number depends on which authority one chooses to believe. For example, the boas and pythons are sometimes split into separate families, the *Pythonidae* and the *Boidae,* and sometimes treated as subfamilies of the *Boidae,*

as here. Since living things do not come with labels, classification is always a matter of debate.

Recently, comparisons of molecular DNA have revolutionized taxonomy, showing that many groupings based solely on physical characteristics may not be valid. The technique is still at the experimental stage, however, and those that are contained in this book are the traditional classifications of modern snakes. In the case of the diverse *Colubridae*, only the major subfamilies have been included.

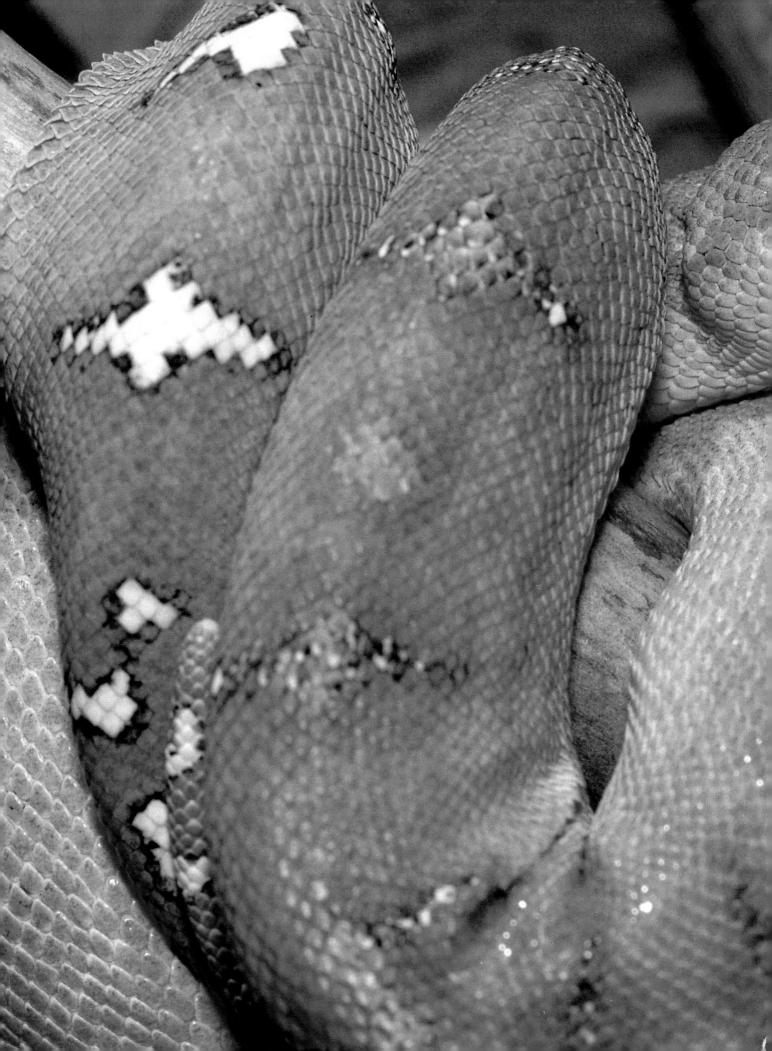

WHAT ARE SNAKES?

BODY STRUCTURE

◆◆◆◆◆◆◆◆◆◆◆◆

What is a snake? It may be easier to say what a snake is not. It is not a legless lizard, although biologists believe snakes arose from ancestral lizards millions of years ago, dropping legs, eyelids and external ears along the way. A snake is not slimy, nor is it evil incarnate. A snake is a highly adaptable animal with a unique, ground-level approach to life – an approach that has been extremely successful for millions of years.

Snakes are the most linear of vertebrates, nothing more than a skull and a wildly extended spinal column. Virtually all other vertebrates rely on appendages of some sort for locomotion – wings, legs, arms, flippers, fins – but not the snake. Yet, despite their 'stripped-down' body, snakes have no trouble manoeuvring their way through life.

A snake skeleton is beautiful in both an adaptive and abstract sense. The paired ribs arch out from each vertebra, forming a

LEFT
A snake's skeleton is a marvel of delicacy, as shown by this rattlesnake skull. Note that the reserve fangs, which would normally rest flat against the roof of the mouth behind the main fangs, have been mounted incorrectly.

BELOW
Snakes are the most linear of vertebrates, few more so than the vine snake *(Oxybelis aeneus)* of Mexico and Central America, which lives in the trees, blending in with the twigs and vines.

concave umbrella that runs the length of the snake's interior. A human being has 33 vertebrae, but a snake has hundreds – more than 400 in many of the colubrids. The amount of movement between each spinal segment is limited, but the net effect is an animal that can writhe and coil sinuously, so that even the word we use to describe such shapes is 'serpentine'. Snake bones are delicate and easily damaged; even the skull is made up of many smaller, lightly fused bones, lacking the solidity of a mammalian skull. As we'll see, there are good reasons for this delicacy, but it lends an ethereal air to a snake skeleton.

Each pair of ribs is anchored by muscles to the one in front and behind it. The pair is also attached to a wide belly scute, or scale, part of the overlapping series of ventral scales that covers the undersides of most snakes, and are essential for locomotion. Although the ribs themselves are thin, there is still little room left within the body cavity. Animals are, as a rule, bilaterally symmetrical; that is, appendages and paired organs are the same size, and are positioned opposite each other. Snakes, which have already dispensed with legs, have also broken the rule of symmetry with regard to several internal organs.

Lungs are the best example. Lizards (from which snakes evolved) have two, side by side. Very primitive snakes, like those in the family *Xenopeltidae*, have two lungs, but the left is only about half the size of the right. In pythons and boas, also primitive snakes, the left lung is only one-third the size of its neighbour. In the huge, advanced family *Colubridae*, numbering more than 1,500 species, the left lung has either disappeared or shrunk to a functionless nub. The right lung, on the other hand, has elongated to fill much of the body cavity, doing the work of two. When a snake breathes, its entire body seems to expand and contract with each inhalation and exhalation.

The heart is also somewhat elongated, although not to the extent of the lung or the liver. Like most reptile hearts, the snake's is only partially efficient; it has three chambers (compared to a bird's or mammal's four), and the chambers allow the oxygenated and deoxygenated blood to mix – hardly the ideal situation. More importantly, a snake lacks an effective way of creating and maintaining body heat; that is, it is 'cold-blooded'.

Scientists shy away from the term cold-blooded, and with good reason. A water snake basking in the sun on a warm summer's day may have a body temperature nearly the same as a mammal's. But a mammal or bird can generate body heat, thanks to a metabolic rate nearly four times that of a reptile's, and can regulate its internal temperature with insulating fur or feathers (if the air is cold), or by panting, flushing or sweating (if the air is warm). In scientific terms, birds and mammals are endotherms, whereas a snake is an ectotherm, meaning that its

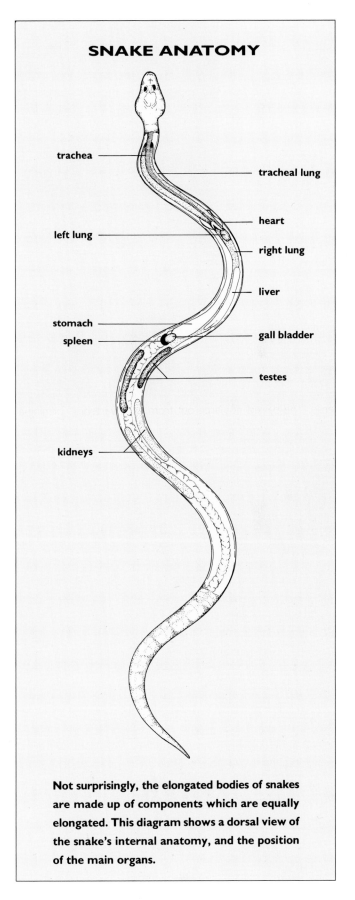

SNAKE ANATOMY

trachea

tracheal lung

heart

left lung

right lung

liver

stomach

gall bladder

spleen

testes

kidneys

Not surprisingly, the elongated bodies of snakes are made up of components which are equally elongated. This diagram shows a dorsal view of the snake's internal anatomy, and the position of the main organs.

RIGHT
Snakes are ectotherms –
'cold-blooded' animals –
and must regulate their
body temperature by
moving from sun to
shade. This northern
water snake *(Nerodia
sipedon)* has just emerged
from hibernation in early
spring.

body temperature is regulated by the surrounding environment. That basking water snake, for instance, must be careful not to let its body temperature rise much above 100 or 105°F (38.1 or 40.9°C), or else it risks heat-stroke and death. On a sunny day, snakes will move from sun to shade repeatedly, trying to keep their thermal level just right; in hot deserts, they may burrow into cooler sand. In chilly weather, snakes will be sluggish, and if the temperature drops too low they fall into a torpor and may die. An endotherm under similar conditions might shiver to produce more body heat, but an ectotherm like a snake is at the mercy of the weather.

With this in mind, the world-wide distribution of snakes is no surprise; they are most common in tropical and warm desert environments, less so in temperate zones and all but absent from the highest latitudes and altitudes. In the tropics, blessed by constant high temperatures the year round and, just as importantly, at night as well as during the day, snakes can be active with little concern for the weather, ensuring only that they avoid direct, midday sun.

The story is different in temperate regions. Here, night-time temperatures even in midsummer may fall below the optimum levels for snakes. (This is especially true in alpine zones or deserts, where cooling is pronounced at night.) Snakes often begin each morning by basking, to raise their internal temperature to a suitable degree, and they may congregate at night in areas that

retain solar heat. This behaviour is most obvious in the desert, where macadam roads stay warm long after the sun has gone down. Herpetologists and collectors know that the best way to find snakes on a cool desert night is to drive slowly along back roads, looking for those soaking up the last of the heat.

As autumn progresses and the thermometer slips, temperate-region snakes must spend more and more time basking each day against the chilly air. Winter, when it arrives, would be fatal to snakes exposed above ground, so they retreat to hibernacula, or hibernation dens, from early autumn onwards. Some species of snakes may travel a significant distance to return to traditional denning sites, which must offer flood-free quarters below the frost line – the reason snakes are absent from the permafrost zone of the Arctic.

Denning congregations can be quite large, and may include more than one species of snake, frequently a mix of venomous and harmless types. The den may be an old mammal burrow, like that of a woodchuck, or a deep crevice in a boulder-strewn slope, an anthill, a sawdust heap or rotting tree stump. Most dens face south for maximum warming. Because the snakes arrive weeks before they must actually begin hibernation, the area around a communal den may literally be 'crawling with snakes', to the horror of passers-by. Denning sites are often the scene of mass slaughter and indiscriminate collection, and because one den may protect most of the snakes for a large area, such sense-

LEFT
Tolerance of cold varies
from species to species.
The common garter
snake *(Thamnophis
sirtalis)* is one of the
hardiest, emerging weeks
earlier in the spring than
many other varieties.

RIGHT
Red-sided garter snakes
*(Thamnophis sirtalis
parietalis)* gather by the
thousands at limestone
sinkholes in parts of the
northern United States
Plains, one of the greatest
examples of mass denning
by snakes.

FAR RIGHT
Direct sunlight can be as
dangerous to a snake as
extreme cold. This New
Mexico ridge-nosed
rattlesnake *(Crotalus
willardi obscurus)* must be
careful not to bask in the
fierce south-western sun
for too long.

less actions can decimate local populations. Some of the largest communal den sites known are used by red-sided garter snakes (*Thamnophis sirtalis parietalis*) of the northern Plains of the US. Each autumn hundreds of thousands gather at limestone sinks, providing a moving carpet – and a remarkable spectacle for those lucky enough to witness it.

Hibernating snakes are not sleeping, as is often thought – their body temperature simply drops so low that function becomes impossible; respiration and heartbeat become almost nil. If the temperature should dip below freezing, the snakes risk death. Many die regardless, for although their metabolism is diminished, it does not halt, and those individuals who enter the winter den without sufficient fat reserves may starve. According to one study, as many as 40 per cent of all northern water snakes (*Nerodia sipedon*) perish during hibernation.

The end of hibernation is as gradual as its start. The snakes stay close to the den for several weeks, retreating underground in the event of a late cold snap. Some species are more cold-tolerant than others, and so appear much earlier in the spring. Garter snakes, for example, are very hardy and may even be found sliding through the slush of a spring snow, while copper-heads and timber rattlesnakes in the same area will not venture away from their dens until weeks later.

Extremely hot weather is just as dangerous to snakes as cold, and in regions where midsummer is a time of scorching drought, many snakes estivate; that is, retreat into a den to wait for cooler temperatures. In some species, estivation appears to be in response to a lack of water, rather than heat.

SKIN, SCALES AND MOULT

◆◆◆◆◆◆◆◆◆◆◆◆◆◆

To those who have never touched a snake, and are finally coaxed to stroke one, the response is almost always the same – 'It's not slimy!' Snakes are not eels, and their skin by nature is completely dry, smooth or rough as the case may be.

Like all reptiles, snakes are protected by a layer of horny scales growing out of the skin, which may hide the skin completely from view. When a snake swallows a big meal, however, the skin stretches and is easily visible between the scales. Scales come in a wide variety of shapes, sizes and textures; there is even a scale, called the brille or spectacle, that covers the lidless eye. The body scales of boas have microscopic ridges that reflect light like a prism, giving the snakes a shimmering iridescence. Coral snake scales are extremely smooth and glossy, a feature reproduced faithfully in the many species of milk snakes that mimic them.

A great many species have keeled, or ridged scales, giving them a rougher appearance; the garter snakes and water snakes are common examples, but there are other species that take this style of scale to a higher degree of development. The rough-scaled tree-viper (*Atheris hispidus*) of East Africa is covered with scales that stand out from the body at a sharp angle; in addition,

the head scales have such a pronounced keel that they are tent-shaped. It may be that the bristly scales help break up the snake's shape in the trees it inhabits. Another arboreal snake, the bush viper (*A. squamiger*) has similar but less heavily keeled scales.

Snake scales come in a wealth of textures, patterns and colours. These examples are from a north-western garter snake (left), boa constrictor (above), Indian (Burmese) python (facing page, above) and rainbow boa (facing page, below).

The bizarre wart snake (*Acrochordus javanicus*) of the Indo-Pacific region lacks normal scales, and is covered — top and bottom — with rough, granular bumps that render its entire body a rasp. An aquatic snake, this species uses its strange scales to capture fish. Lying on the bottom in loose coils, the snake appears to passing fish to be nothing more than an odd rock or stump with inviting nooks and crannies. When the fish tries to squeeze in for cover, the snake tightens, holding the fish with its roughened hide until it can be swallowed.

The outer layer of a vertebrate's skin is dead, and must be replaced as the animal grows. Human skin cells slough off individually as scurf, but reptiles and amphibians shed the entire outer layer at once, at fairly regular intervals. The moult is especially dramatic among snakes.

The process begins with the release of hormones, which trigger the growth of a new layer of skin and scales beneath the existing layer. Once that step is completed, lymphatic fluid is pumped into the microscopic space between the two layers, separating them and causing the eyes to appear milky. During the several days prior to shedding, the snake will be reclusive, avoiding food

and much more irritable than usual (which may be due to an impaired ability to see clearly).

About 24 hours before moulting, the fluid is reabsorbed and the eyes clear. The snake begins to rub its nose against an abrasive surface, until the tiny rostral scale comes loose; the same happens with the mental scale at the tip of the lower lip. Gently rubbing, the snake literally slides out of its old skin, which peels off inside out, like a long sock. The moulted skin is thin and translucent, but retains a hint of colour — and an exact replica of the snake's scale pattern, right down to the eye brille. An experienced naturalist can easily identify the past owner of a moulted skin found in the woods.

A freshly moulted snake is the picture of health; its colours bright and pattern crisp. Occasionally, though, the moulting process will go wrong, the skin will tear and old patches will stubbornly cling to the new; this is especially common around the eyes. In most cases the skin eventually works itself free through abrasion, but infrequently infection will set in, or the skin will be permanently disfigured. Scar tissue from old wounds is often the source of such trouble.

FACING PAGE
A snake's outermost layer of skin is dead, and must be discarded periodically as the snake grows. Beginning at the lips, it peels backwards inside out, revealing the bright, fresh layer beneath. This is a black rat snake *(Elaphe obsoleta)* in mid-moult.

LEFT
About a week before shedding occurs, the snake's lymphatic system secretes a layer of fluid that separates the old skin from the new. This eastern hognose snake *(Heterodon platyrhinos)* has the milky eye of a snake preparing to moult.

ABOVE
Dumeril's ground boa *(Acrantophis dumerili)* is a fairly small, heavy-set boa from Madagascar, an island where deforestation threatens this and many other endemic flora and fauna.

SENSES AND SENSORY ORGANS

◆◆◆◆◆◆◆◆◆◆◆◆◆◆

Sliding through the grass, a snake pauses, flicking its tongue rapidly in and out several times. It turns, still flicking, and strikes into a tussock, coming out with a small frog firmly in its jaws. It is often said that snakes 'taste' the air with their tongues, but this is not, strictly speaking, true. While the tongue is part of a complex sensing system, it does not appear to have highly developed sensory abilities of its own. Delicately forked, it is not built for food manipulation like mammalian or bird tongues. Instead it collects and transports odour particles and chemicals from the air, depositing them in a nerve-rich pit in the roof of the mouth, known as Jacobson's organ. Tied into the snake's nasal passages and sense of smell, Jacobson's organ analyses what the tongue collects, keeping its owner informed of food, predators, water and other vital aspects of the immediate surroundings.

Even when the mouth is closed, there is a tiny opening below the rostral scale through which the tongue can slide, and an active snake will test the air every few seconds, especially if it is hunting or suspicious of danger. A snake that is being handled will often flick its tongue over the hands of the person holding it, but there is no harm – the tongue is not a stinger of any sort.

While human beings are sight-oriented creatures, snakes place a great deal more emphasis on smell and taste. To a snake, if it smells right, it is right – so much so that a hognose snake can be convinced to eat a diet as alien as strips of raw beef, so long as they have been rubbed against its normal prey, toads. Snakes have an impressive ability to use their senses to track down food, although – as with any olfactory system – it is less effective in rain, strong wind or very dry conditions.

LEFT
The tongue of the western terrestrial garter snake *(Thamnophis elegans)*, like that of all snakes, has little sensory ability itself. Instead, the tongue collects chemicals and odour particles from the air and transports them to Jacobson's organ in the roof of the mouth.

FACING PAGE
Many nocturnal snakes, like the lyre snake *(Trimorphodon biscutatus)*, have vertical pupils that open wide at night for better low-light vision.

Snakes have well-developed eyes and apparently see well, although it is hard for us to know for sure. Some tests indicate that colubrids, and possibly other groups, have at least rudimentary colour vision, and some snakes hunt by sight; coachwhips, for instance, 'periscope' by raising their heads high above the ground, scanning for rodents and birds. In most species, however, distance vision appears to be poor.

Literature has had a field day through the years with the snake's 'baleful glance' or 'hypnotic stare', ascribing it to the serpent's supposedly evil character. Of course, any animal that lacks eyelids is going to seem to be staring, but this is no reflection on the snake's demeanour. A number of the more primitive species are virtually blind, the eyes reduced to tiny spots that can do little more than sense the presence or absence of light. At the other extreme are many of the nocturnal snakes, equipped with large, cat-eye pupils that open wide in darkness. Such vertical pupils are also the rule among vipers and pit vipers, as well as many of the rear-fanged colubrids; the long-nosed tree snake (*Ahaetulla prasinus*) of South-east Asia, has long, horizontal pupils that give this bird- and lizard-eater excellent forward vision.

Snakes universally lack an external ear opening, middle ear and ear drum, although they have a sophisticated inner ear for balance. They are deaf to airborne vibration of the sort we hear, but they are very sensitive to vibrations carried through the ground, which they appear to pick up through their lower jaw. Human footfalls are usually enough to send a skittish snake into the undergrowth.

The most highly developed snake sense is found in only one subfamily, the *Crotalinae*, or pit vipers. It is nothing more than a pair of small, forward-facing holes, one on each side of the face between the nostril and eye. These pits are thermal receptors, lined with nerves and extraordinarily sensitive to heat – according to some researchers, capable of discriminating differences of as little as one-tenth of a degree Fahrenheit. Each pit is made up of two chambers, separated by a thin membrane and connected by a muscular tube. Infra-red radiation, emitted by warm-blooded prey, is detected by the pits; subtle differences in intensity and location between the two widely spaced organs allows the snake to triangulate, gauging the distance and angle to its prey, and guaranteeing an accurate strike.

The majority of pit vipers hunt warm-blooded prey, but not all do, and even those that usually eat rodents or birds will also hunt reptiles and amphibians on occasion. Copperheads (*Agkistrodon contortrix*), for example, feed to a great extent on frogs, toads and salamanders – animals that do not give off much of a thermal image. But because the facial pits are so sensitive, the copperhead can apparently detect the slight difference between a frog's body temperature and the temperature of the background, sensing what might be described as a 'heat void' where the frog is. Hot or cold, the snake has a target.

Boas and pythons have a cruder version of this heat-seeking method, in which thermoreceptive pits have evolved between the labial scales along lips. The principle, however, is exactly the same. The best example is the emerald tree boa (*Corallus canina*) of South America, which has nearly two dozen large openings on each side of the head, all aimed forward to sense the presence of the tropical birds and arboreal mammals. The green tree python of Asia, which has evolved convergently with the tree boa, has a smaller set of labial pits on the top jaw only, and has an effective range of about a foot and a half.

LEFT
Pit vipers are considered the most advanced group of snakes, largely because of their heat-sensing facial pits, shown here on a yellow-phase timber rattlesnake *(Crotalus horridus)*.

FACING PAGE
Pit vipers, like the copperhead *(Agkistrodon contortrix)* have a number of senses that can be brought to bear on prey, including the odour-collecting tongue and heat-sensing facial pits.

MOVEMENT

◆◆◆◆◆◆◆◆◆◆◆◆◆◆

For animals without limbs, snakes get around very well. In fact, there is virtually no place that a legged animal can go, that a snake cannot follow – on or below the ground, through the water and into the trees. There is even one species that can glide through the air.

Most of the time, snakes move across the ground with what herpetologists call lateral undulation – the typical S-curves that come to mind when we think of snakes. The outer edges of the curves anchor the snake's body, allowing it to push forward; this is graphically demonstrated by a snake track in sand, which shows the soil heaped up at the outside of the curves. Occasionally, most snakes use what might be called an 'earthworm crawl',

a slow-motion way of getting from one point to another. The head and neck probe forward a short distance, then anchor the body while the rest of the snake's length is pulled up.

On very loose sand, snakes may have to resort to sidewinding, in which they throw loops of their body forward at an angle, keeping most of their belly off the ground. Even when one watches a snake sidewind, it is difficult to understand just how it is able to move. The body is aimed almost 90 degrees from the direction of travel, and the tracks left behind are a series of separate fish-hook marks, rather than a continuous line. Sidewinding has been compared to walking, since only a small part of the body touches the ground at any given time.

RIGHT
A rough green snake
(Opheodrys aestivus)
perches in a blooming
redbud tree, pausing in its
hunt for insects. The
rough green snake spends
much of its time in trees,
while its close relative,
the smooth green snake
(O. vernalis) stays mostly
on the ground.

The large ventral scales on the belly, which overlap like roof shingles, provide the means for another sort of movement, effective only on rougher surfaces. In a beautifully co-ordinated fashion, the rib pairs connected to each scale move the plate forward fractionally, grip and pull the body along; to an observer, it appears that ripples of movement are flowing along the snake's underside, like the motion of a caterpillar. Large, heavy snakes are especially good at this rectilinear creeping, as it is known, but even small specimens will employ it on occasion.

Snakes are masters of using the slightest irregularity in the ground as a base against which to move. The most remarkable examples are rat snakes and milk snakes that can climb large trees, even those in which the trunk is too wide to coil around. Instead the snakes climb by using a form of rectilinear movement, gripping with their ventral scales the tiniest bumps and ridges in the bark.

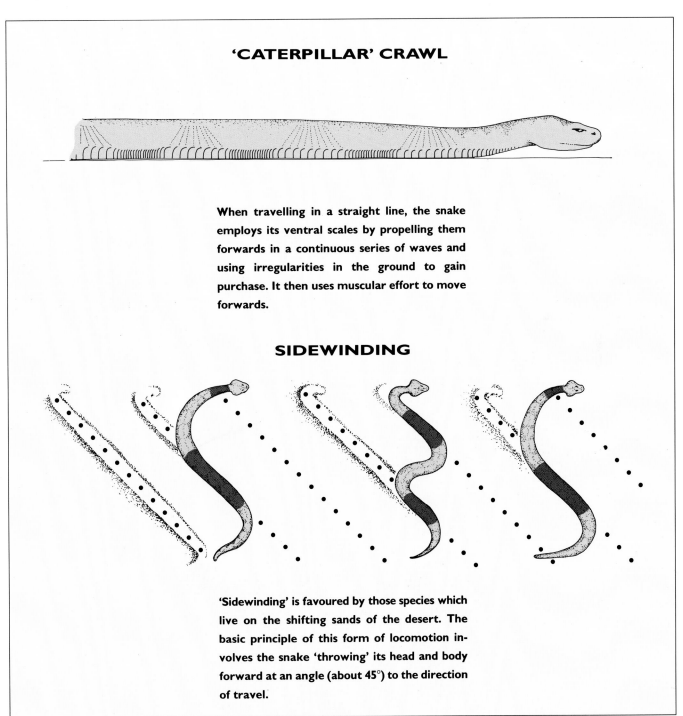

'CATERPILLAR' CRAWL

When travelling in a straight line, the snake employs its ventral scales by propelling them forwards in a continuous series of waves and using irregularities in the ground to gain purchase. It then uses muscular effort to move forwards.

SIDEWINDING

'Sidewinding' is favoured by those species which live on the shifting sands of the desert. The basic principle of this form of locomotion involves the snake 'throwing' its head and body forward at an angle (about 45°) to the direction of travel.

SERPENTINE MOTION

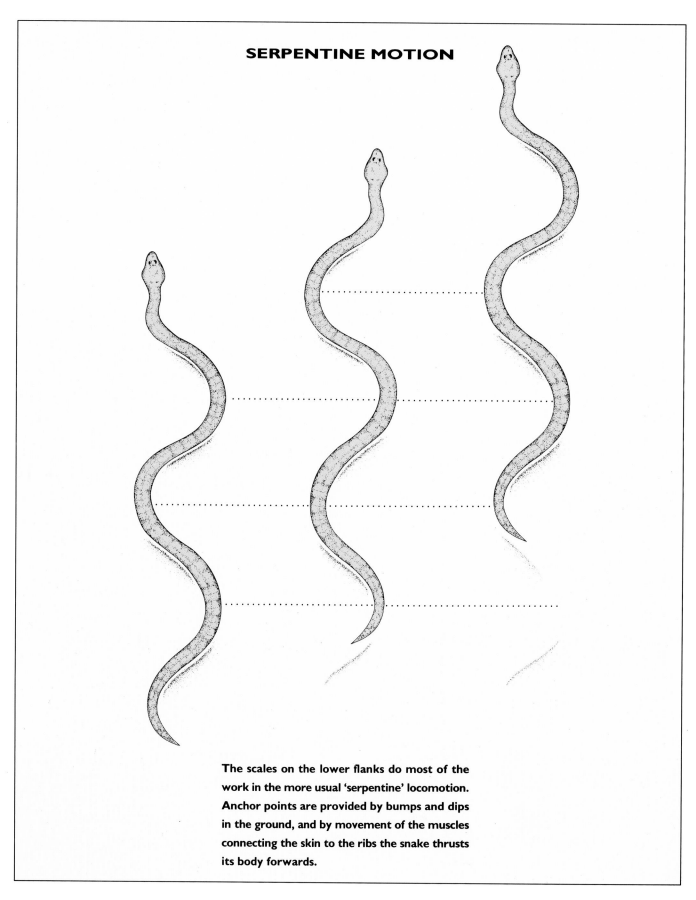

The scales on the lower flanks do most of the
work in the more usual 'serpentine' locomotion.
Anchor points are provided by bumps and dips
in the ground, and by movement of the muscles
connecting the skin to the ribs the snake thrusts
its body forwards.

LEFT
LEFT
Moving across the ground in typically 'snakey' loops, a western ribbon snake (*Thamnophis proximus*) demonstrates lateral undulation, a common form of locomotion among snakes.

In the treetops, snakes may take one of two approaches to bridging the gap between branches – either by becoming extremely long and slim, or staying somewhat shorter and developing a prehensile tail. Many of the most arboreal species have gone the slender route – snakes like the parrot snake (*Leptophis ahaetulla*) of Central and South America and the venomous twig snake (*Thelotornis kirtlandii*) of Africa. The blunt-headed tree snake (*Imantodes cenchoa*) of the Neotropics, a rear-fanged species, has special vertebral supports jutting out to the sides that provide rigidity to the body, so that the snake can ease more than half its body into empty space with little trouble.

Prehensile tails are found among many of the neotropical and Asian pit vipers, and tree-dwelling boas and pythons, and provide their owners with a solid anchor, although these snakes tend to be much less agile and slower-moving than the slim tree snakes. The oddest adaptation to life in the trees is found in the Asian flying snakes of the genus *Chrysolopea*, which can parachute from tree to tree thanks to an expandable rib cage.

Old stories often talk about snakes chasing human beings – false on several accounts, since snakes are almost universally shy. More to the point, a person can outwalk most snakes, to say nothing of outrunning them. A big snake like a racer or a coachwhip, moving quickly through the underbrush, may appear to be going very fast, but in truth it cannot go faster than four or five miles per hour, and most snakes are a lot slower than that.

All snakes, however, have very fast reaction times, and can spin and strike at a predator with blurring speed. The belief that a snake must coil to strike is another in the long string of unfounded myths; while many do coil first, a snake can bite regardless of its position, and many strikes are made with the neck in a simple S-curve. Non-poisonous snakes can and do bite defensively, instantly letting go, unlike a feeding strike in which they hang on to their prey. The curved teeth make U-shaped rows of punctures, and if one pulls back during the bite they may leave rows of deep scratches, but there is little that is dangerous about the bite of an average-sized non-poisonous snake.

LEFT
The huge, upcurved rostral scale of the Pima leaf-nosed snake (*Phyllorhynchus browni*) helps it burrow through sand. Biologists have noticed that this snake's distribution closely matches that of the creosote bush, in the south-western United States.

EVOLUTION AND DESCENT

◆◆◆◆◆◆◆◆◆◆◆◆◆◆

nakes, with their thin, delicate bones, are a paleontologist's nightmare. Even the skull (which, in mammals, is the bone most often preserved over time) is lightweight and easily destroyed by natural forces. Consequently, there are relatively few snake fossils. Enough have been found, however, to determine that snakes are the youngest branch of the reptiles, having appeared only about 150 million years ago; by contrast, lizards have been around for more than 250 million years, and turtles even longer.

There is also little doubt that snakes developed from lizards, which to this day have a tendency to lose their legs when circumstances dictate – the 'glass snake' of the South-east of the United States is a good example. It resembles a snake superficially, but has a movable eyelid and an external ear opening. Glass lizards spend quite a bit of time burrowing, but also hunt above ground. The sand skink of Florida shows an even greater adaptation to a subterranean life, and while it is not an intermediate to snakes, it suggests the way the snake's ancestors may have diverged from lizard stock.

The sand skink is small, only about 5in (12.7cm) long. The legs are all but gone, leaving only minute stubs that used to be forelegs. Since the sand skink spends most of its time underground, it has lost its external ear canal, and its eye has degenerated and is covered with a transparent scale in the eyelid.

It seems likely that snakes developed in much the same way, from lizards that evolved for a burrowing life. The legs were lost, since they would interfere with tunnelling. The ear channel was sealed off to keep out dirt, and the bones of the ear, rather than connecting to an ear drum, instead joined the lower jaw, the better to sense soil vibrations. The unique structure of modern snakes' eyes suggests that the organs nearly vanished among

LEFT
The anal spurs on an Indian (Burmese) python *(Python molurus bivittatus)* are a visible link to all snakes' evolutionary past, since the tiny nubs are the remnants of hind legs.

ancestral snakes, then re-evolved when snakes once more took to the surface and needed vision.

The clearest evidence that snakes were once limbed comes from the pythons, boas and blind snakes, three primitive families. Hold a male boa and you'll quickly discover two horny projections near the vent; these are the visible remnants of hind legs, part of a vestigial pelvic girdle that remains hidden inside, an echo of the snake's past. Obviously no use for walking, the spurs do serve a practical purpose, helping the male stimulate the female during courtship.

The primitive snakes also share another lizard-like trait – two functioning lungs. As mentioned, in more advanced snakes the left lung has degenerated to the point of uselessness, and several other paired organs – the kidneys, and in some cases even the oviducts – have been reduced from two to one. The advantage, of course, is to squeeze the internal organs into the snake's streamlined form.

The blunt-headed tree snake, several feet long and barely thicker than a pencil, shares the South American rainforest with the anaconda (*Eunectes murinus*), a boa that may exceed 250lb (113.5kg) and 25ft (7.6m). The range of snake species is astonishing – over 2,500 have been identified, and more undoubtedly exist in poorly explored tropical regions. A few species are found within 400 miles (644km) of the Arctic Circle in central Canada, and the European adder (*Vipera berus*) is actually found within the Arctic itself in the Soviet Union. There are wholly aquatic sea snakes and a host of desert species. They range from primitive blind snakes to the advanced, fairly intelligent pit vipers and elapids.

While the diversity of snakes numbers only about one-third of bird species, it is remarkable if viewed from the typically human perspective that a legless, deaf, cold-blooded animal is somehow inherently inferior. The snakes, by their very success, put the lie to that argument.

ABOVE
The boas and pythons are considered primitive snakes for several reasons, including the structure of their skulls, vestigial hips and only partially reduced left lungs. This is the rough-scaled sand boa *(Eryx conicus)*, which is native to Africa.

SNAKE ECOLOGY

◆◆◆◆◆◆◆◆◆◆◆◆◆◆

Snakes do not exist in a vacuum: they are part of an intricate, dazzlingly complex web of interrelationships between plants, other animals and the inorganic environment. At their most basic, these interrelationships revolve around food – who eats what, and is in turn eaten by what. Snakes are of course predators, but with very few exceptions they are not what ecologists call 'top-order consumers', at the pinnacle of the food chain. Most can be categorized as somewhere in the middle, being both predator and prey.

The majority of snakes are predatory generalists, taking a wide variety of prey, depending on what circumstance and chance bring their way. This is a safe path to follow, from an evolutionary point of view, because the snake can take advantage of whatever prey base happens to be the most abundant. A garter snake, for instance, can focus its hunting on frogs and toads in early spring, when the amphibians are concentrated in breeding ponds, then switch to earthworms when the ground warms enough to bring them to the surface at night, later in the summer. A gopher snake (*Pituophis melanoleucus*) can switch from mice and voles to bird's eggs and chicks during the peak of the nesting season, then return to a mammalian diet after the birds have finished breeding. The catholic tastes of most snakes is exemplified by the black racer (*Coluber constrictor*), which according to one study ate 32 per cent reptiles, 26 per cent small mammals, 18 per cent birds and bird eggs, 15 per cent insects and 9 per cent amphibians. A snake with such a diet is unlikely to starve.

LEFT
More than 5ft (1.5m) of Sonoran whipsnake (*Masticophis bilineatus*) drapes itself across the branches of a mesquite tree, where it is hunting lizards and birds.

FACING PAGE
The egg-eating snakes of the genus *Dasypeltis* are famous for their habit of swallowing bird's eggs much larger than their heads. This southern brown egg-eating snake (*D. inornata*) could easily handle an egg twice as large as the one it has swallowed.

While most snakes are dietary generalists, there are some species that have taken the opposite approach, focusing on one specialized food source. At face value this may seem like a riskier strategy, placing all one's eggs in a single basket, but specialization is common in nature, and has some distinct advantages. A generalist is competing against many of the other generalists for the same, admittedly wide, food supply. By focusing on a single food source, a specialist can eliminate much of the competition with other species. The danger, naturally, is that if the food source dries up, due to ecological changes, disease or human interference, the specialist is in trouble.

There are not nearly as many dietarily specialized snakes as there are generalists. One is the thirst snake (*Dipsas variegata* and related species), a South American colubrid that appears to eat almost nothing but snails. Getting a snail out of its shell is a difficult task, since the mollusc can close the entrance with a tight-fitting operculum. The thirst snake does so by using its shorter upper jaw bone as a brace, then forcing its longer lower jaw into the shell around the operculum, pulling out the snail's body and swallowing it. Because their diet is so soft, thirst snakes lack the expandable chin flaps found on most snakes, and they cannot therefore swallow large prey.

There are other specialists. An African relative of the thirst snake feeds exclusively on slugs; the African egg-eating snake (*Dasypeltis scabra*) subsists almost wholly on freshly laid bird's eggs; and the cat-eyed snake (*Leptodeira annulata*) of South America eats the eggs of leaf frogs. Hognose snakes (genus *Heterodon*) of North America specialize in toads and, to a lesser degree, frogs; queen snakes (*Regina septemvittata*), also North American, eat nothing but freshly moulted, soft-shell crayfish. Two unrelated snakes – the neck-banded snake (*Scaphiodontophis annulatus*) of Central America and the African wolf snake (*Lycophidion capense*), a rear-fanged colubrid – have specialized teeth to help them catch and hold skinks, lizards with notoriously smooth scales. The wolf snake has somewhat enlarged teeth that are recurved, as with most snake teeth, but the neck-banded snake's teeth have become flattened and knife-like for holding its slippery prey.

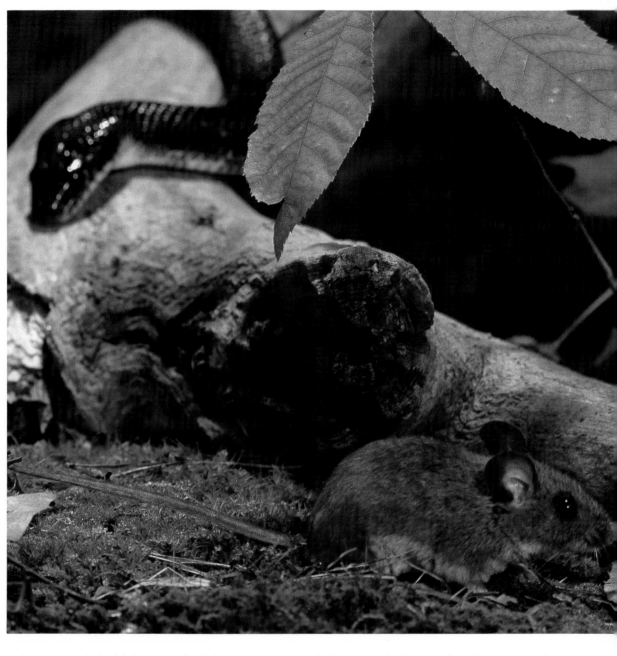

FACING PAGE, ABOVE
Eastern hognose snakes *(Heterodon platyrhinos)* specialize in hunting toads, and are not put off by the toad's toxic skin secretions. The snake, in turn, uses a mild venom to quiet its prey while swallowing. Despite the venom, hognose snakes are completely harmless to human beings.

FACING PAGE, BELOW
One of the strangest food specialities among North American snakes is that of the queen snake *(Regina septemvittata)*, which eats almost nothing but soft-shell crayfish.

RIGHT
Snakes are part of the complex web of interrelationships between plants, animals and the physical environment. A black rat snake *(Elaphe obsoleta)* hunting a white-footed mouse may itself become a meal for a hawk, heron or weasel.

Every living thing occupies an ecological 'niche' – not a physical space, but the combination of its habitat, lifestyle and feeding habits that determines its place in the natural community. Each species has a slightly different niche, to avoid direct competition; if two species try to occupy the same niche, one will invariably displace the other, a phenomenon known to zoologists as competitive exclusion.

Natural selection continually refines a creature's adaptations to its particular niche, and in the process reduces the chances of direct competition, especially for food. Even very similar species make their living in subtly different ways. On the surface, a black racer *(Coluber constrictor)* and a black rat snake *(Elaphe obsoleta)* are pretty much the same – both generalists that take a variety of mammals, birds, reptiles, amphibians and invertebrates. Both are big, exceeding 5 or 6ft (1.5 or 2m); both even look very much alike. But the racer, while capable of climbing, spends most of its time on the ground, whereas the rat snake is well known for the amount of time it spends hunting through the trees. Similar snakes – different lifestyles.

Only the very largest of the constrictors are safe from predation, and even then, a hungry jaguar or cayman may be tempted to attack despite the risks. For smaller snakes, violent death is an ever-present danger, from a myriad of sources. Snakes may be eaten by large fish, big frogs, predatory lizards, by mammals,

birds or other snakes; hatchlings face additional dangers from such invertebrate hunters as large spiders and scorpions. In the tropics, columns of army ants pose a hazard for small snakes that cannot quickly get out of their way – and those that try to flee may be caught by birds that have learned to follow the columns, picking off the escapees.

In the south-west of the United States, one of the most ardent snake hunters is the greater roadrunner, a large, ground-dwelling cuckoo. Roadrunners do not eat only snakes (they also take large numbers of lizards, bird nestlings, rodents and insects), but they do not hesitate to kill even rattlesnakes if the chance presents itself. Legend to the contrary, roadrunners do not corral rattlers with a circle of cactus spines, then wait for the snake to skewer itself; the bird depends on a sharp beak and excellent reflexes to avoid being bitten.

Another legendary snake hunter is the mongoose – and again, legend far exceeds truth. While a mongoose will kill snakes, including the venomous elapids, it does not seek out such prey, nor is it immune to cobra bites, as is often claimed (but it is more resistant to the venom than most mammals, however). Several of the world's dozen species of mongoose have been introduced to new areas in the hope they would eliminate dangerous snakes; in every case, the mongooses have largely avoided the snakes in favour of mammals and ground-nesting birds, driving several species to the brink of extinction in the process.

Some snake predators have developed a degree of immunity to the venom of the species on which they frequently feed. African meerkats have a resistance to spitting cobra venom, but not to adder venom; Virginia opossums, on the other hand, have a tremendous resilience to rattlesnake toxin, but none at all to

cobras, which do not occur in the New World. Kingsnakes, which feed to a large degree on snakes, and occasionally on rattlesnakes, have functional immunity to pit viper venom; the same is true for the South American mussurana, which preys heavily on neotropical pit vipers.

Human beings can be among the most efficient of snake predators, although any large-scale destruction is likely to have unintended side-effects. In areas where snakes have been severely reduced, crop losses to rodents often skyrocket, since snakes are among the world's greatest ratters. In many parts of the tropics, people have overcome their fear of snakes, encouraging certain species around their homes for pest control. These are not always harmless species, either, for example, the Wagler's pit viper (*Tropidolaemus wagleri*) of Indonesia is considered a good luck charm around houses, where it keeps rodents in check.

Snakes have not been studied to nearly the same degree as birds, and much of their life history remains unclear. The size of home ranges, for example, a critical bit of information if we are to understand how snakes live, is known for only a handful of species. The majority seem to spend their lives within a few acres; predictably, large, active snakes like racers and rat snakes appear to have greater ranges than more sedentary species such as water snakes.

In areas where suitable winter dens are scarce, snakes may make travel several miles between their hibernacula and summer territories. This is known to be the case in some areas for racers, and canebrake rattlesnakes (*Crotalus horridus atricaudatus*) are thought to move as much as 19 miles (30.5km) away from their winter dens – a remarkable feat, if true. Likewise, a marked juvenile eastern garter snake (*Thamnophis sirtalis*) dispersed almost 10 miles (16km) from its hibernacula.

By no means do all snakes have fixed home sites. Timber rattlesnakes and copperheads apparently do not establish permanent summer ranges, but simply wander in a vaguely circular path during the warm months, ending up back at the den again in autumn.

There is little evidence that snakes are territorial, and the combat dances that occur between male pit vipers apparently have more to do with dominance and breeding than the defence of hunting grounds. This is interesting, because lizards, from which snakes evolved, are highly territorial, and have developed a wide array of crests, dewlaps and spines to help bluff intruders of their own species.

FACING PAGE
Black racers *(Coluber constrictor)* are dietary generalists. This hatchling will feed on insects and tiny amphibians, adding a wide variety of reptiles, birds and mammals as it grows.

LEFT
According to one study, canebrake rattlesnakes *(Crotalus horridus atricaudatus)* may travel as much as 20 miles (32km) between summer feeding grounds and their winter dens.

DEFENCE

◆◆◆◆◆◆◆◆◆◆◆◆◆◆◆

A snake's most obvious defence is its tooth-studded mouth, which in many species is tipped with poison. As effective as biting may be, it is not the only defence a snake can offer – it may also try frightening displays, unexpected colours, hideous odours, loud noises and outright deceit. And for all that, the most effective defence is probably simple flight.

Almost all snakes will bite if provoked, although there is a world of difference between what constitutes provocation for different species. Adult northern water snakes (*Nerodia sipedon*) are known for their foul tempers, although young specimens are easily tamed. Ring-neck snakes (*Diadophis punctatus*), which are so small they could do no damage anyway, rarely ever try to bite, and hognose snakes are also long-suffering. Milk snakes and rat snakes may try to bite when first captured, but with time and frequent handling become almost affectionate.

Although ring-neck snakes do not bite when handled, they often secrete a liquid that stinks all out of proportion to the snake's small size. Anal glands are common in snakes, and many can discharge a yellowish or greenish fluid when picked up or attacked. This musk is strong-smelling and utterly vile if it gets into the mouth; a dog that picks up a rat snake in its teeth is apt to drop it immediately, then go looking for water, leaving the snake in peace. The musk is long-lasting, and it takes plenty of soap and water to rid one's hands of the smell after exposure. Many snakes, while musking, will twine into a ball or figure-8, smearing the substance over most of their body; while this may be coincidence, it is hard not to believe the snake is instinctively spreading its protection around. One species, the Chinese stink snake (*Elaphe carinata*) relies on musk to a greater degree than do most snakes. The anal glands in this yellow and brown rat

LEFT
Temperament varies from species to species, and between individual snakes. The northern water snake *(Nerodia sipedon)* is generally an aggressive biter, but occasional individuals are very docile, and can be safely handled immediately after capture.

LEFT
The Sinaloan long-nosed snake *(Rhinocheilus lecontei antonii)* has an especially foul anal discharge that it throws towards intruders by slashing its tail in the air.

BELOW
Hidden among the leaves of a staghorn sumac, a rough green snake *(Opheodrys aestivus)* all but vanishes.

snake are very large, and the fluid they produce is even more noxious than usual.

Given a choice, snakes will flee the scene when confronted with danger; only under the most unusual conditions do they ever advance towards an enemy. Being so thin, snakes can literally melt into the scenery, slipping through tiny cracks and down holes, disappearing into rodent tunnels in the grass or under loose rocks. Most snake sightings are of the hind end – and even that vanishes a moment or two later.

Movement is a giveaway in nature, though, and snakes often stay put, relying on their natural camouflage, a very effective defence. Camouflage can take many forms, from the standard cryptic coloration most people think of when they hear the word, to disruptive patterns and countershading.

The snake world is full of examples of cryptic coloration; that is, colours and patterns designed to match the background. Some are simple, straight-forward schemes, like the rough green snake (*Opheodryus aestivus*) of the East United States, which is bright green to match its leafy surroundings. Other snakes seem woefully miscoloured, if seen out of context. A boa constrictor (*Boa constrictor*) photographed on a green lawn looks almost garish,

ABOVE
The Avicenna viper *(Cerastes vipera)* of the Middle East and Africa lacks the sand-blocking supraocular scales of its close relative the horned desert viper, but shares its camouflaging pattern.

covered as it is with rusty saddles, buff blotches and swirls of yellow. In its natural habitat, though, the snake matches exactly the dull browns of dead rainforest leaves, and the trickles of sunlight filtering through the treetop canopy. The Gaboon viper (*Bitis gabonica*) is another species with a flamboyant pattern that merges seamlessly with its natural habitat.

Just as brilliantly coloured birds are surprisingly difficult to see in the shadows and half-light of the rainforest, so too, are some tropical snakes. The yellow morph (or colour phase) of the eye-lash palm-pitviper (*Bothriechis schlegelii*) is about as easy to overlook as a neon sign – but not when the snake is curled among the ripe yellow fruit of a palm tree, where it hunts for lizards and small birds.

Copperheads (*Agkistrodon contortrix*) are among the most highly camouflaged of North American snakes. The irregular hour-glass marks of chestnut and tan blend among the fallen oak leaves of eastern forests with uncanny accuracy. The author once pointed out a copperhead, lying several feet off the trail, to two hiking companions. After five minutes of visual searching and repeated descriptions of where to look they still could not see the snake, until it was gently prodded with a long stick and moved slightly.

head than in most snakes – protrude above the surface. In addition to providing camouflage, the sunken snake benefits from the markedly cooler temperatures just underground.

Desert vipers the world over, including the sidewinder (*Crotalus cerastes*) have large, eyebrow-like supraocular scales above the eyes. The most pronounced belong to the horned desert viper (*Cerastes cerastes*) of Africa and the Midddle East whose scales rise up and back like thickened fangs. The 'horns' are not for defence, but keep sand from piling up and covering the eyes when the snakes are partially buried.

Cryptic coloration is easy to understand, but other camouflaging patterns may not seem as logical, although they are equally effective. Disruptive patterns, like a tiger's stripes or a killdeer's breast bands, break up an animal's outline. The long lateral stripes found on garter snakes, ribbon snakes, queen snakes and others serve the same purpose, making it harder for a predator's eye to register the form of the snake. Many of the kingsnakes (genus *Lampropeltis*) employ disruptive coloration, but here the pattern is crossbarring rather than lengthwise stripes. Several species have distinct white bands or chain markings, which fragment the snake's outline against the surroundings.

When camouflage fails, some snakes change tactics completely by making themselves very visible. The ring-neck snakes, among others, are dull above but bright yellow, orange or red below. If

Not surprisingly, desert snakes are usually coloured to match the sand, in shades of tan or grey. Most are also rough-skinned, with strong keels on each scale – another layer of camouflage, since a glossy, shiny snake would be easy to spot against the sand, and with little vegetation in the desert for cover, snakes are always at risk from birds that can spot them from long distances.

Some of the Old World desert vipers are masters of disguise. The Peringuey's viper (*Bitis peringueyi*), or dwarf sand adder, is coloured to match the sands of the Namib Desert in south-western Africa. Its behaviour more than its coloration, though, keeps it out of sight. When not actively hunting, the viper will vibrate its body rapidly, sinking beneath the surface of the sand until only its eyes – which are positioned much higher on the

FACING PAGE, BELOW
Given away by its choice of backgrounds, this yellow-phase of the eyelash palm-pitviper *(Bothriechis schlegelii)* would vanish in a clump of ripe, yellow palm fruit.

TOP
Frightened, a prairie ring-neck snake *(Diadophis punctatus arnyi)* displays its coiled, brightly coloured tail. The sudden flash of colour may startle predators, and fool them into concentrating on the snake's tail, rather than its vulnerable head.

RIGHT
The flashy colours of a Texas coral snake *(Micrurus fulvius tener)* are a clear warning to predators that the snake is dangerously venomous.

threatened, they often abruptly curl the tail into a corkscrew, revealing a sudden flash of colour. It may be that the unexpected appearance of so odd a colour startles birds. (The coil looks a great deal like a large eye, and birds have been shown to be scared by artificial eye spots on moths.) It may also be that the bright tail focuses the predator's attention on the least susceptible part of the snake's body; concentrating on the tail, the bird might not notice the snake heading for a hole until the coil suddenly vanishes underground. Among frogs and insects, such sudden displays are called 'flash marks', and they are also found in such snakes as red-bellied snakes (*Storeria occipitomaculata*) and black swamp snakes (*Seminatrix pygaea*).

There are snakes that make no attempt to hide themselves – indeed, they make every effort to be as visible as possible. Brightly splashed with red, yellow or orange, they broadcast an implicit warning with their colours. The coral snakes of the New World, for example, are highly venomous, and it is in their best interest to let potential predators know it. There are more than 50 coral snake species, each with a distinctive series of red, black and yellow or white bands. Over thousands of generations, birds have learned to avoid snakes with those colours, so that many snake-eating species now have an instinctive fear of anything marked in red, yellow and black (including wooden dowels painted by scientists for experiments).

FACING PAGE
In a display of Batesian mimicry, the harmless scarlet kingsnake (*Lampropeltis triangulum elapsoides*), a subspecies of the milk snake, almost perfectly imitates the Texas coral snake's warning pattern, and gains protection in the process.

LEFT
The hood of an angry cobra is a flap of skin stretched over specially adapted ribs. The cobra can raise or lower the hood at will.

In the nineteenth century, Henry Walter Bates, one of the pioneering naturalists in the Neotropics, first noticed that many harmless, edible species of animals mimic dangerous or unpalatable varieties, thus coming under their umbrella of protection. This Batesian mimicry, as it is now known, is especially prevalent among a number of harmless colubrids, particularly milk snakes, that share the forest or desert with coral snakes. In the South and South-west United States, the impostors can safely be told from true coral snakes by the sequence of colours; in coral snakes the yellow and red touch, while in milk snakes black separates the two. This is not the case in the tropics, where there are many more varieties of coral snakes with an almost endless variation of colour sequences.

But why are all the coral snakes patterned so similarly? Close relation is not the answer, since many snakes within the same genus look nothing like one another – and coral snakes comprise three genera, not one. The answer may be a second type of mimicry known as Müllerian mimicry after another nineteenth-century scientist, Fritz Müller. According to Müller, when two toxic species resemble each other, they reinforce the protection each possesses. By all looking generally alike, the coral snakes present a unified front, of sorts, and the snake-eating birds need to learn only one pattern to avoid all of them.

Snakes are not the only animals to mimic other snakes. The caterpillars of several North American swallowtail butterflies are green, and bulbous in the front with a pair of orange eye-spots that imitate a snake; if attacked, they can extrude an orange, fleshy prong that resembles a snake tongue. An even more faithful snake mimic is found in the American tropics, where there is a large moth caterpillar whose underside copies a small arboreal pit viper, right down to the bulging 'eyes', which even have tiny white flecks to resemble highlights. When attacked, the caterpillar turns half its body over, revealing the copy.

The Asian pipesnakes (family *Aniliidae*) have taken both flash colours and Batesian mimicry and combined them into a unique defensive behaviour. When threatened, the snake buries its head under its body coils, and raises its spatulate tail, which is banded with black, white and red. The tail curves forward and is waved about, making a passingly good imitation of an angry cobra with its hood spread. Obviously, the ruse would be worthless unless the local predators knew what a cobra looked like, and that it was to be avoided. A true cobra's hood is a dramatic warning. At ease, a cobra looks much like any other snake, but when aroused, muscles in the neck tighten, raising ribs inside the hood and causing it to flare. The size and shape of the hood varies by species. The monocled cobra (*Naja naja*) of Asia and the Cape

RIGHT
The threat display of a bullsnake *(Pituophis melanoleucus sayi)* is enough to make most predators reconsider. The snake rears back in tight curves, opens its mouth and emits a piercing combination of snorts and hisses.

cobra (*Naja nivea*) of Southern Africa have two of the largest and best-developed hood styles, while the various spitting cobras and the water cobra have small, narrow hoods. The king cobra (*Ophiophagus hannah*), the world's largest venomous snake, is another with a very narrow hood.

Hoods and swollen necks aren't unique to cobras. Many other species, most harmless, use the same technique to make themselves appear bigger and more threatening than they are. The hognose snake (*Heterodon platyrhinos*) found in the eastern United States employs a very wide, brightly coloured hood as part of its elaborate bluff act, which includes close-mouthed strikes, hissing and feigning death. The hood is not a case of mimicry, since North American predators cannot be expected to know what an Asian cobra looks like. The boomslang (*Dispholidus typus*), one of Africa's deadliest snakes, inflates its throat like an inner tube when agitated, as does the twig snake (*Thelotornis kirtlandii*).

Loud hissing has a immediate effect on potential enemies, particularly when combined with false strikes or other threat displays. The bullsnakes of the genus *Pituophis* specialize in this defence. When approached, they pull back in a series of S-curves, with the head raised well off the ground. Inhaling, they swell with air, then open their mouth and begin to hiss – an incredibly loud noise for the size of the snake, accentuated by a small knob in front of the glottis that partially blocks the flow of air. Like the hognose snake, in the United States the northern pine snake (*P. m. melanoleucus*) is sometimes known as the 'hissing adder', while a western subspecies, the bullsnake (*P. m. sayi*) gets its common name from the loud snorts that accompany its hissing.

Many snakes rapidly vibrate the tips of their tails when upset, producing a dry buzzing in the leaves that is distressingly similar to the warning of a rattlesnake. While this could be a form of auditory mimicry, tail-buzzing is found in such venomous species as copperheads as well as harmless snakes, and some scientists

LEFT
The rattles of a rattlesnake are horny segments, each loosely connected to each other. When shaken rapidly, they make a dry, buzzing sound.

believe the sequence of development is really the reverse – that tail-buzzing led to rattles, not the other way round. According to this theory, rattlesnakes were once rattle-less, like all the other pit vipers. Since the core of their distribution is the American Plains and South-west – once the home to immense herds of grazing mammals – the theory contends that the rattles evolved as a way to warn off bison and other big animals that would otherwise trample the snake underfoot, even if one or two were bitten in the process. If tail-buzzing is a common behaviour in many snakes, as seems to be the case, the theory makes sense. It is reinforced by the existence of the Catalina Island rattlesnake (*Crotalus catilienensis*), which lives in an secluded habitat with no grazers, and has only a silent, horny button instead of an articulated string of rattles. Protection from grazers has also been suggested as an explanation for the spitting cobras of Africa.

A rattle is an effective warning device, if the snake chooses to use it. A startled rattler may strike with no warning, and temperament varies from individual to individual, even within the same species. Some rattle at the slightest provocation, while others will bite first and sound off later.

A rattlesnake's rattles, incidentally, are no indication of age, as is so often thought. A new segment is added with each moult – and moults may occur several times a year, depending on the temperature, condition of the snake and how often it feeds. Further complicating matters, the rattle is fragile, and the segments easily pull apart.

If rattles are a complex, highly evolved defensive mechanism, many snakes get along quite well with the barest minimum. Ball and burrowing pythons (*Python regius* and *Calabaria reinhardtii*) are masters of the tuck-and-wait strategy. When danger is near, they roll into a ball, stick their heads in the centre and wait it out. It isn't fancy, but it works.

BELOW
The Catalina Island rattlesnake *(Crotalus catilinensis)*, a small western form, has lost its rattle string, apparently because its island home had no large mammals to warn off.

LEFT
The rattles of this black-tailed rattlesnake *(Crotalus molossus)* are a blur as it sounds a warning. Rattlesnakes do not always rattle before a strike, nor will they invariably bite after rattling; usually the sound alone is enough to frighten intruders away.

FEEDING

◆◆◆◆◆◆◆◆◆◆◆◆◆◆

All snakes are strictly carnivorous, and as mentioned previously, there is scarcely a form of animal life on which one species of snake or another does not prey. The few reports of snakes eating vegetable matter, for example the python discovered with mangoes in its stomach, probably represent cases of mistaken identity.

Because of its shape and physiology, a snake has hurdles and advantages not found in other creatures. A bird is highly mobile when it hunts, and because it can move quickly over a wide area, a bird can subsist on small prey, even though its metabolism is far more demanding than a snake's. The snake, on the other hand, is limited in its hunting range, certainly when compared to a bird or a mammal. The snake moves relatively slowly, and opportunities to catch food come along far less frequently than to a songbird. With its slow metabolism that is no real problem for the snake, which can go for extended periods (in some cases months) without eating. The flip side of the situation, however, is that the snake must make the most of each meal; in order to survive, it should be able to eat the biggest prey it can possibly catch.

If a snake's head were constructed like a human being's, it wouldn't be able to eat anything thicker than its neck – indeed, because it cannot chew, it would be restricted to swallowing long, thin prey like worms (and many snakes do, in fact, get by on just this kind of diet). But snakes have an evolutionary advantage that allows them to swallow animals much wider than themselves. Their heads, quite literally, go to pieces when they eat.

The bones of our head are firmly attached to each other: the lower jaw hinges in place just below our ears, and is rigidly joined in the front; the upper mandible is fused into a solid chunk of bone. Our lower jaw drops open about 45 degrees, but that is all. If a mammalian skull is built for strength, a snake skull is a marvel of delicacy: lightly constructed and loosely connected. When a snake eats, cartilage joints stretch open at the front of the upper and lower jaws, while special hinges at the back of the lower mandible allow the rear of the jaws to swing wide, like a gate. The mouth opens nearly 150 degrees as it expands to nearly twice its normal size, ready to accommodate a hefty meal. The neck skin, in turn, is exceptionally elastic.

THE FLEXIBLE JAW

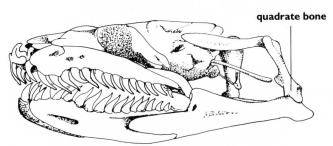

quadrate bone

SNAKE JAW CLOSED

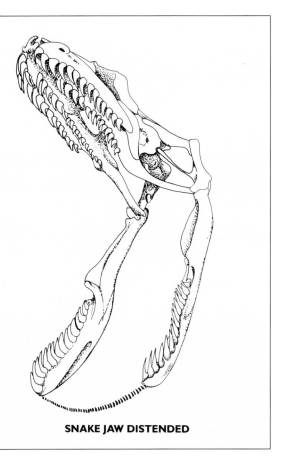

SNAKE JAW DISTENDED

A versatile jaw enables snakes to swallow their food head-first and whole, even when the prey is larger in diameter than the snake's body, and may even be alive and struggling. The quadrate bone, connecting the lower jaw loosely to the skull, works like a double-jointed hinge so that the snake can drop its lower jaw at the back of its mouth as well as the front. Sharp curved teeth hold the quarry in place while the snake seems to 'walk' its gaping mouth forward around its food.

RIGHT
Caught raiding the corn store, a mouse disappears down the gullet of a black rat snake *(Elaphe obsoleta)*, a fabled rodent hunter.

FACING PAGE
Poisonous snakes have evolved individualized toxins that are most effective against their common prey. The venom of the Asian mangrove pit viper *(Trimeresurus purpureomaculatus)* stops birds and small mammals.

LEFT
A western coachwhip
(*Masticophis flagellum
testaceous*) 'periscopes'
above the grass on a
Texas barrier island.
These large, agile snakes
often hunt by sight, a
generally rare form of
behaviour.

A snake's teeth (aside from fangs) are fairly simple: short, backward-curving and very sharp. They are designed merely to grip and hold, something they do well, but they lack cutting surfaces, and cannot chew or chop the prey into smaller pieces. It must, therefore, go down whole, and since the snake lacks feet with which to push the food down its gullet, it must have some way to force the food into its throat. The special structure of the head is again the answer; the two sections of the upper jaw work independently of each other, and the rows of teeth (two sets, one around the rim of the jaw and another on the roof of the mouth) alternate to 'walk' the prey down the throat.

Swallowing large prey can be a lengthy and difficult process, and may last for more than an hour. With its mouth plugged, the snake needs a way to breathe. It does so by extending the glottis, a tubelike organ embedded in the floor of the mouth, around the prey. The glottis is the perfect breathing tube, bypassing the food until it disappears down the throat.

Once down the hatch, the length of time it takes for the food to digest depends – as does so much in a snake's life – on the air temperature. The snake usually seeks out a warm spot out of direct sunlight, and rests quietly while its stomach breaks down the meal. Just how long the digestive process takes also depends, obviously, on the size of the meal, and a large, bulky prey item may be visible for several days or longer.

Most snakes are happy to eat live food; the frog in a garter snake's belly may squirm and heave for a time after the meal is complete. But a few groups of large snakes kill their prey immediately before eating – by constriction or envenomation.

Popular belief aside, a constrictor does not 'crush' its prey; the process is much more refined than an exercise of simple, brute strength. Constricting is a speciality of the boas, pythons and a large number of the colubrids, such as rat snakes and kingsnakes, although non-constrictors like garter snakes will occasionally twine around their prey to help hold it during swallowing.

LEFT
As shown by this impressive skin, the bushmaster *(Lachesis muta)* is a very big snake. In fact, this native of Central and South America is the longest pit viper in the world.

SWALLOWING PREY

Having killed it with a massive dose of venom, a timber rattlesnake *(Crotalus horridus)* eats a mouse.

Prey that is first killed may be inspected closely for several minutes, the snake flicking its tongue over the body to search for the head. Once found, swallowing begins here, thereby avoiding the possibility of legs or wings catching on the jaws (1). Throughout the feeding process, the snake's mouth is completely filled, and in order to

3

breathe, its muscular windpipe is pushed forward on to the floor of the mouth.

As the victim's larger body parts enter the mouth, the lower jawbones become detached from the quadrate bone, enabling the jaw to open at the back as well as the front (2). The snake's curved teeth act as hooks, holding the prey in position, while the left and right sides of the jaw move forward, pulling it in (3).

Rippling motions in the anterior third of the body force the prey into the stomach (4), while a few 'yawning' motions indicate that the jawbones are being reconnected – signalling the end of the meal.

4

RIGHT
The fox snake *(Elaphe vulpina)* of the Great Lakes region in the US is, like all the rat snakes, a powerful constrictor, killing its prey by suffocation.

FAR RIGHT
Two drops of yellow venom appear at the ends of a rattlesnake's fang during a 'milking' procedure. Snake venoms are among the most complex biochemical substances in the world, and while they make many snakes dangerous to people, their most important function is killing food.

A true constrictor usually strikes near the head or forequarters of the prey, grabbing hold and not letting go. Instantly, the snake throws one or two coils around the animal's midsection and tightens, but the idea isn't to crush the prey, but to suffocate it. With each exhalation of the captured animal, the coils squeeze more closely around the rib cage, preventing the prey from breathing freely; often the snake will open its mouth, once the coils are set, and grab the smaller animal by the head, completely cutting off the air supply. While constriction usually is a fairly quick procedure, large prey like a crocodile or cayman may struggle for prolonged periods. The snake simply waits, taking in the slack in its coils. Only when the prey is dead, or nearly so, does the constrictor relax its body and begin to feed.

The power of even a small constrictor's body is impressive – a six-foot (2m) black rat snake, wrapped tightly around a person's forearm, can squeeze with startling strength, and has the ability to kill a rat, squirrel or small rabbit. The biggest constrictors, the Old World pythons and the anaconda, have been known to kill deer, antelope, goats and pigs. There are many anecdotal tales of large, wild constrictors killing people, and a few cases (most involving children) have been reasonably authenticated, but even the giants pose no serious threat to humans, despite decades of television 'explorers' rolling in the muddy shallows with big anacondas. Bear in mind that in such cases it was the human that picked the fight for the camera, not the snake.

Even more elegant than constricting is the capture of food through envenomation. This fact seems to get lost in the hysteria over poisonous snakes, but their venom is only tangentially for defence. Its prime function is a way of killing prey, not people.

ABOVE
A copperhead *(Agkistrodon contortrix)* bares its fangs in a strike. This specimen has an unusual, striped pattern which is only occasionally seen.

LEFT
Many of the elapids, such as the coral snake *(Micrurus fulvius)*, possess neurotoxic venom that attacks and disables their victims' nervous systems.

Snake venom is a marvellously complex substance – or rather, group of substances, since there are almost as many venoms as there are venomous snakes. A more detailed treatment of poisonous snakes and their relationship to humans follows (see *Venomous snakes and snake bites,* page 74), but for now it is enough to know that there are two major groups of venomous snakes – the families *Elapidae* and *Viperidae.* The *Elapidae* are the so-called 'front-fanged' snakes, the cobras, kraits, coral snakes, sea snakes and their allies, all of which possess venom that works strongly on the prey's neural system. The *Viperidae* – the true vipers and the pit vipers – generally have venom that destroys tissue, particularly the circulatory system.

For snakes, use of venom solves a sticky problem. A snake is a rather delicate creature, and grappling with a bigger, sometimes heavier animal armed with teeth or claws is a risky enterprise. Ribs can be broken, spines can be severed, serious wounds may be inflicted. With venom, however, the snake need only strike – a split-second's contact, instantly broken, and the stunned prey wanders off to die. The snake merely bides its time, follows the scent or heat trail to its quarry, and settles down to a quiet – and harmless – meal.

The largely hemotoxic (blood-poisoning) venoms of the *Viperidae* have an added benefit for the snake – the hemorrhagic compounds of the venom kill by breaking down body tissue, so the prey is already being 'digested' before it is even swallowed. Animals that have been injected with venom, experiments show, are digested more quickly than those killed by researchers and presented to the snake already dead. Human beings who are bitten by snakes with hemotoxic venom may suffer days of severe pain and swelling, depending on the species, but the prey animals for which the venom is designed are so overwhelmed by the flood of toxin that most die within minutes.

REPRODUCTION AND COURTSHIP

◆◆◆◆◆◆◆◆◆◆◆◆◆

The great leap between amphibians and reptiles was the eggshell, which made the conquest of dry land possible. Despite their scaleless skin, many amphibians survive away from water – in fact some toads are able to live in deserts – but for reproduction, they still require standing water, or at least a very humid environment. Spadefoot toads in the arid Great Basin of the United States must wait underground for a rare storm to fill the temporary pools and puddles, so that they can enter a frenzy of breeding. Their eggs are gelatinous, and out of the water they quickly dry and perish.

In the same region lives the Great Basin gopher snake (*Pituophis melanoleucus deserticola*), a large constrictor and, like the spadefoot toad, an egg layer. The gopher snake's eggs are different, however. They are larger, even taking the relative size of the parents into account, and there are far fewer of them than the toad's. The toad's survival strategy is to produce large numbers of eggs in the hope that a few will survive desiccation, competition and predators. The oblong snake eggs, on the other hand, have fewer obstacles to maturity, so the female gopher snake can invest greater resources in each, endowing them with a substantial packet of yolk.

What makes this possible, to a great degree, is the almost watertight shell of the snake egg, which prevents the embryo from drying out. The shell is leathery and supple, unlike the rigid shells of bird's eggs, but like a bird's, the snake's egg has microscopic pores that connect the embryo with the outside world. A membrane layer known as the chorioallantois disposes of gaseous carbon dioxide while taking in oxygen, and reduces water loss to the external environment. It is not a perfect system. While the wastes from the growing embryo are safely converted to uric acid and stored away in the egg, the metabolized yolk of a reptile egg produces little water, and a snake egg laid in a very dry place will quickly shrivel and die. Birds have solved this problem with an even more watertight shell, and a fatty yolk that produces lots of metabolic water, but reptiles must pick the spots for their eggs with great care.

LEFT
Frogs' eggs are typical of amphibian eggs – gelatinous and prone to desiccation, and therefore usually laid in standing water.

FACING PAGE
Snake eggs have a leathery shell and are much more resistant to drying than frogs' eggs. These hatchlings are Florida pine snakes (*Pituophis melanoleucus mugitus*).

Egg-laying snakes most often seek out damp, warm places in which to lay their eggs. More than one gardener in the United States, forking up a load of compost or old manure for the vegetable patch, has uncovered a stash of rat snake eggs. The site is a logical choice, since the rotting vegetation provides both moisture and a stable, relatively high temperature that accelerates the eggs' development.

The vast majority of female snakes lay their eggs and immediately forget about them. Parental care is all but unheard of – with a few notable exceptions. Most of the pythons will remain coiled around their clutch of eggs through the development period, and the Indian python (*Python molurus*) even produces constant muscular spasms, which raise the body temperature slightly and help incubate the 100 or more eggs.

While most egg-laying snakes take advantage of naturally occurring heaps of vegetation, the king cobra (*Ophiophagus hannah*) is the only species in the world known actually to construct a nest. The massive female uses her body to pull dead leaves and ground litter into a pile, then forms two chambers, one on top of the other – a lower room for the eggs, and an upper layer for herself, where she remains to guard the eggs through the incubation period. The female bushmaster (*Lachesis muta*) of Central and South America is also said to defend her nest site – in an aggressive manner.

Regardless of the level of incubative care, when hatching comes the baby snakes are on their own. Equipped with a sharp, temporary 'egg tooth' that juts out the front of the mouth, the infant slices through the shell and enters the world. Even among the

RIGHT
A baby black rat snake
(Elaphe obsoleta)
emerges from its buried
egg. Just visible at the
front of the mouth is the
tiny egg tooth, which will
fall off shortly after
hatching.

FACING PAGE
Two Sonora coachwhips
*(Masticophis flagellum
cingulum)* twine about
each other during
courtship. Such sociability
lasts only during the brief
courtship session, and
after mating the snakes
go their separate ways
again.

pythons and king cobra, the females take no role in caring for the hatchlings, which are fully functional from the moment of birth, able to hunt and eat with no help. Venomous snakes hatch with operating venom glands, and can give a dangerous bite shortly after hatching.

While a marked improvement on the amphibian method, reptilian egg-laying still has its drawbacks. During the development period, which may last for months, the eggs are exposed to a multitude of hazards – desiccation, flooding, infection by fungi or bacteria, and perhaps worst of all, destruction by sharp-nosed predators like raccoons or opossums, which relish reptile eggs. Some snakes have improved the odds for their offspring by dispensing with egg-laying altogether. They are the viviparous snakes, the live-bearers.

The advantages in live-bearing are obvious; the young indirectly benefit from the female's ability to defend herself, and are not sitting targets for weeks on end. There is a cost to the female, who grows bloated and slow-moving during the gestation period, and may cease eating entirely through the three or four months it lasts. One might expect viviparous species to bear fewer young than the egg-layers, but the opposite is frequently true; an average-sized eastern United States garter snake (*Thamnophis sirtalis*) is capable of bearing 40 or more babies.

In mammals, the growing foetus is connected to the mother via a placenta, a membrane composed of both foetal and maternal tissue, through which nourishment passes to the foetus, and waste materials are carried away by the mother's bloodstream. Even viviparous snakes do not have so finely honed a system; in some the eggs are merely retained inside the body, without shells, and the babies are born as they 'hatch'. In other, more advanced snakes like the pit vipers, the infants are encased in what might be termed a pre-placenta, since the sac appears to allow for a limited exchange of gases and nutrients.

Labour, when it comes, may last for hours. Each baby first appears as a lump moving down the female's abdomen, becoming more pronounced as it reaches the vent; the female lifts her tail slightly, and the baby snake, encased in a transparent membrane, slides out. The adult makes no attempt to help the infant, which quickly breaks out of the sac. Depending on the species, the babies may immediately crawl off, or they may stay near their mother for a day or two. The female timber rattlesnake (*Crotalus horridus*) may even defend her brood for a few days.

LEFT
Unlike most snakes, female timber rattlesnakes stay with and guard their broods for a day or two, after which the family splits up, never to rejoin.

A RATTLESNAKE GIVES BIRTH

Live-bearing among snakes reaches its most refined state in the pit vipers. Here, heavy with unborn young, a female timber rattlesnake *(Crotalus horridus)* begins the slow process of birth (1).

Coiled tightly, an infant rattlesnake slides the last inches towards freedom, producing a lump in the female's tail

1

2

Female copperheads (*Agkistrodon contortrix*) and timber rattlers are both known to gather in loose concentrations known as breeding rookeries, which are used year after year. The rookeries are often near the winter den, although how the young find the den is not known. Timber rattlers, like many temperate-zone live-bearers, only give birth in alternate years. Once the babies are born and dispersed the female feeds heavily, trying to recoup the reserves she lost in gestation – reserves she will need to make it through hibernation.

Courtship, among reptiles, is not as flashy as that of birds who make use of songs and their bright plumages. Externally, the sexes are identical in colour and pattern, although female snakes often have a tail that tapers more sharply below the vent than in males. Scent apparently plays a large role in bringing the sexes together – an obvious course for creatures both solitary by nature and highly attuned to odour. The females of many species

3

as it approaches the vent (2), and is pushed by muscular contractions out of its mother.

Free of the cloaca (3), the baby rests for several minutes, still encased in the pre-placental sac; this membrane provides a limited link between the embryo and the mother, although not the complete bond found in mammals (4).

As the membrane starts to dry, the young rattler breaks free of the case. Completely self-sufficient, it will nevertheless stay with its mother and eight or nine siblings for a few days before the family disperses.

4

lay down a scent trail, which amorous males follow to its source. (Male garter snakes may also lay down a mock pheromone trail to confuse rivals.) Once together, there may be a great deal of rubbing, poking and stroking of the female by the male, who eventually twines around her, bringing their cloacas together for mating. Fertilization is internal.

Among many pit vipers (especially rattlesnakes) and quite a few colubrids, two individuals may twine, then raise the front halves of their bodies off the ground, braced against each other for support. For years, this was assumed to be a courtship ritual, until someone bothered to check the sex of the participants. In every case, both were males. Far from courtship, the 'combat dancing' is a form of pre-mating aggression, presumably to determine dominance, and perhaps to decide which males can breed. There is still much to be learned about the life history of even the most common snakes.

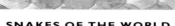
VENOMOUS SNAKES AND SNAKEBITES

◆◆◆◆◆◆◆◆◆◆◆◆◆

Only about one-third of the world's snakes are venomous to human beings, and only a portion of those pack enough punch to kill a person. According to some estimates, one's chances of dying from snakebite in the United States are 15 or 20 times less than the chance of being killed by lightning. Driving a car down a busy road is far more hazardous than walking through even a 'snake-infested' rainforest. Still, there is a fascination with anything that has the power to reach through our insulated, civilized world and kill us. Even people who are repulsed by snakes find them morbidly interesting, ready to believe any flight of fancy.

The toxicity of most snake venoms is greatly overrated. Only a handful of species have venom strong enough to kill human beings in a majority of bites, and many of those, like the sea snakes, rarely come in contact with people. For example, the venomous snake that lives in closest proximity to most of North America's human population – the copperhead – has a very mild toxin, and the timber rattlesnake, while more dangerous, rarely causes fatalities. In fact, not every snakebite results in envenomation. According to one study in Papua New Guinea, 73 per cent of all snakebite victims showed no signs of poisoning, and another in Malaysia recorded 53 per cent of cobra bite victims with no

LEFT
The copperhead
(Agkistrodon contortrix)
is the most widespread
venomous snake in the
eastern half of the United
States, but although it is
frequently common near
homes and towns, bites
are relatively rare and
deaths almost unknown.

FACING PAGE
Handling any venomous
snake, even with a long
snake hook, is a job best
left to experts.

serious envenomation. By some estimates, only a quarter of the people bitten by venomous snakes suffer serious poisoning.

The reason is that venom production is time-consuming, and it makes sense for a snake to husband its supply for use in food-gathering, venom's main purpose. Snakes seem to be able to control the amount injected during a bite, and many strikes result in what is known as a 'dry bite' – one in which little or no venom was injected. Folklore has often held that baby snakes are more venomous than adults. While research suggests this may be true in some cases, it may also be that young snakes have not yet learned to control themselves, and so empty their venom reserves at each bite.

RIGHT
The boldly marked monocled cobra *(Naja naja)* is one of Asia's most dangerous snakes. Ironically, the much larger king cobra, found in the same region, causes far fewer deaths because it is usually shy and unaggressive.

LEFT
A number of colubrids, like the night snake *(Hypsiglena torquata)* of the western United States and Mexico, are equipped with grooved, rear teeth and a crude venom gland system. Rarely dangerous to people, the rear-fanged snakes must chew in order to envenomate their prey.

RIGHT
The prairie rattlesnake, a subspecies of the western rattler *(Crotalus viridis),* is a common snake in the arid grasslands of the American West.

The glands themselves come in several kinds. Those of elapids, vipers and pit vipers are found between the eye and the rear of the jaw, and consist of venom-producing cells and a small holding sac that is connected to the fangs. In rear-fanged colubrids, the venom is produced by Duvernoy's gland, and seeps down grooved teeth into the wound. For this reason, most rear-fanged snakes must chew in order to envenomate. The world's longest venom glands are found in a peculiar group of Asian snakes, known appropriately as long-glanded snakes (genus *Maticora*). The glands of these elapids extend nearly half the length of the snake's body.

It may be that many of the colubrids which are regarded as harmless may in fact be toxic. Many seem to have at least mildly venomous saliva that is effective against their normal prey, if not human beings. Several water and grass snakes of the former genus *Natrix* have been shown to have slightly toxic secretions; in the United States the northern water snake (*Nerodia sipedon*) has an anticoagulant in its saliva, and the European ringed snake (*Natrix natrix*) secretes venom that is fatal to amphibians and small mammals. While these common snakes pose absolutely no danger to human beings, an Asian genus, the keelbacks (*Rhabdophis*), have caused serious envenomation in people.

Once the venom is produced, it needs a delivery system. The colubrids display the most rudimentary approach, at most a set of grooved teeth that are slightly longer than the rest of the set. (Their position in the back of the mouth is suitable for killing prey in the process of being swallowed, but it does no good for killing animals that are not already subdued.) Fangs at the front of the mouth are the next step. Elapids have fixed fangs up front, which are short of necessity so the mouth can close. In cross-section, elapid fangs appeared to be folded into a hollow tube, with a tiny opening at the rear near the tip. The most advanced system of venom delivery is found in the vipers and pit vipers. Their fangs are long and curved, hinged near the top so they can fold flat against the roof of the mouth until needed, and encased in a fleshy sheath. Spare fangs rest against the upper jaw, ready to swing into place. Because the fangs are so much longer than those of elapids, the viperids can deliver their venom more accurately, and deeper into the tissue of their prey.

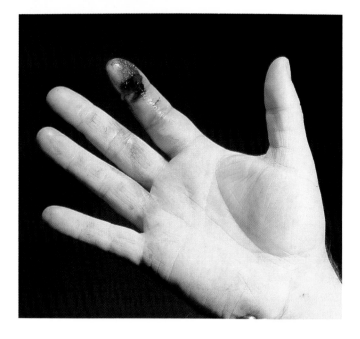

FAR LEFT
Slow-moving unless provoked, the puff adder *(Bitis arietans)* packs a powerful wallop, with a venom that is especially destructive to tissue.

LEFT
March's palm pitviper *(Bothriechis marchi)* is a nocturnal, treetop hunter in the tropical forests of Honduras, killing small birds, lizards, frogs and rodents with its venom.

BELOW
A newly hatched timber rattlesnake *(Crotalus horridus)* bears a silent 'prebutton'. The snake's first moult will reveal a second segment, and for the first time, the baby rattlesnake can display its trademark warning.

FACING PAGE, BOTTOM
Painful but not life-threatening, a copperhead bite causes swelling and bleeding as the toxin's enzymes begin breaking down the nearby tissue. Other venoms are more virulent – and may be deadly.

The title of 'most dangerous snake in the world' is an impossible one to award. It is more than simply a matter of the toxicity of the venom (which often varies greatly within a given species). Just as important is the normal dose, the abundance of the snake, its temperament, how frequently it comes in contact with people, even the percentage of people within its range who go about barefoot, and are thus more susceptible to snakebite. Further muddling the picture, most experimental work on venom toxicity has been done with rats and mice, which undoubtedly react differently from human beings. It is no surprise, therefore, that the snakes that account for the greatest number of human fatalities are not necessarily those with the strongest venom. The bushmaster *(Lachesis muta)*, the world's biggest pit viper, can inject up to 500 milligrams of venom in a bite, but it kills far fewer people in Latin America than the smaller – but more prevalent – fer-de-lance *(Bothrops asper)*, capable of injecting a maximum of about 200 milligrams in a bite.

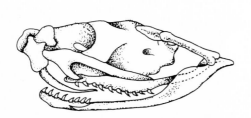

RIGHT
Snakes suffer greatly from habitat destruction, and nowhere is this problem more severe than in the tropics. Extensive deforestation endangers all tropical life, including the hognose viper *(Porthidium nasutus)* of Central America.

HOW A VIPER RELEASES VENOM

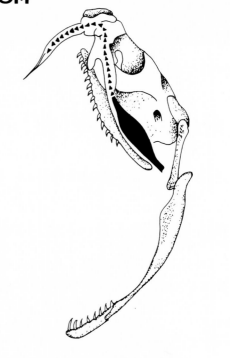

When a pit viper prepares to strike, its long fangs, which have lain flat along the roof of its mouth (1), are swung into position (2), and can be plunged into the victim's neck with one swift jab of the snake's head. As the fangs sink in, muscles contract and squeeze a venom gland in each cheek, forcing the poison out through a narrow tube that runs from gland to fang.

LEFT
The international trade in rare snakes has pushed many species towards extinction, and resulted in global regulation. Many collectors now rear snakes in captivity, with increasing attention given to albinos like this ghostly Burmese strain of the Indian python *(Python molurus bivittatus)*.

BELOW
The San Francisco garter snake *(Thamnophis sirtalis tetrataenia)*, one of the loveliest of North American snakes, is also a federally protected endangered species, having lost much of its limited habitat to development.

RIGHT
In many areas, rattlesnakes like the western diamondback *(Crotalus atrox)* are still the objects of fear, legally unprotected and subject to uncontrolled slaughter.

FACING PAGE
A large timber rattlesnake *(Crotalus horridus)*, taken from its habitat and displayed at a rattlesnake 'hunt' in the Pennsylvania hills, is somewhat luckier than southern and western rattlesnakes that are summarily killed after the round-ups. Even when released, however, the rattlesnakes often suffer from injury and stress that may be fatal.

Death by snakebite is a rare occurrence in most of the world; only in underdeveloped countries of Asia, Africa and Latin America is it a serious danger, and even there the top rate is less than 40 per 100,000 people. Prompt medical care can save most snakebite victims, but such quick treatment is often lacking in rural communities, where folk-remedies like herbs, concoctions of snake brains and incantations are the traditional standbys. Considering that many bites are dry, and many more result in sublethal envenomation, it is perhaps no wonder that the folk-remedies are seen as rather successful.

The standard treatment for snakebite is a shot of antivenin, a serum made by injecting tiny quantities of venom (a tenth or less of the fatal dose) into horses. Over time the dosage is increased until the horse has built up an immunity to the venom; thereafter, the horse's blood supply can be tapped, and the serum, rich in antibodies that destroy the raw venom, is processed out. Freeze-dried, the antivenin can be reconstituted quickly if needed, and injected into the victim. (First, however, the doctor must run an allergy test. A few people are highly sensitive to horse serum, and the allergic reaction can be more dangerous than the snakebite itself.) As risky as it may be, a few people have intentionally built up a degree of immunity to certain snake venoms by injecting themselves with gradually increasing dosages. Quite a few primitive snake cults tried for the same effect by eating snakes or drinking their venom. This last course is not as foolhardy as it sounds, at least for most viperid venoms, which are broken down by stomach enzymes. Elapid venom, on the other hand, is almost as dangerous taken orally as when injected.

MISCONCEPTIONS ABOUT SNAKES

◆◆◆◆◆◆◆◆◆◆◆◆◆◆◆

No other group of animals carries such a heavy load of human misconceptions, legend and tall stories as do snakes. The only thing more remarkable than the wild stories told about them is the fact that so many people believe them. Most 'common knowledge' about snakes, like the belief that they are slimy, is false. Snakes do not hypnotize their prey, suck milk from sleeping cows, sting with their tail (or tongue), swallow their young for protection, or blow poisonous vapours when hissing. They cannot roll in hoops or jump into the air to bite a person's face. Cowboys who trusted to a horsehair tethering rope to keep rattlesnakes out of their bedroll occasionally found them-

selves sharing their warm bedding with an unwanted guest, who had absolutely no hesitation about crossing the rope.

Sometimes there is a germ of truth behind the old myths, like the claim that a snake, regardless of how badly mangled, will not die until sunset. Like most reptiles, snakes have a nervous system capable of involuntary twitches long after death, and people have been bitten by the freshly severed heads of venomous snakes – not because the decapitated head is still 'alive', but because the nerves in the head responded to the stimulus of a touch with a convulsive snap. If a pregnant viviparous snake is killed and cut open shortly before she would have given birth, her abdomen

RIGHT
Eastern hognose snakes *(Heterodon platyrhinos)* hiss as part of their bluff performance, but the air they blow is not poisonous, as is often claimed.

FACING PAGE
Milk snakes *(Lampropeltis triangulum)* haunt barns to catch mice and rats, not to suck milk from cows.

RIGHT
The strongly patterned
Great Basin rattlesnake
(Crotalus viridis lutosus)
is one of the many
subspecies of the
widespread western
rattlesnake.

would be full of living, perfectly formed young. To a frontiersman, the logical explanation is that she swallowed the babies. But 'eyewitness reports' of snakes opening their mouths and allowing their brood to crawl inside are pure fiction.

Milk snakes got their name from the erroneous belief that they creep into barns and steal milk from the udders of cows. Lacking lips, snakes cannot suck, nor is their digestive system adapted for eating a liquid diet. Milk snakes are rodent hunters, and there are no better places to find rats and mice than a barn – the real reason they are common around livestock. And certainly, no cow is going to suffer in silence should a snake clamp its mouthful of teeth onto so sensitive an area as the udder.

A persistent belief in many parts of the world is that snakes mate for life, and that when one is killed, the other stays nearby looking for its mate (or, according to variations on the myth, the survivor goes looking for the killer with revenge in its heart). Snakes are not social, and except for the transitory courtship that is over within hours, they do not remain paired. The exception may be the king cobra, but it is unlikely that even this species has such fidelity to its mate.

As to hypnosis, many small animals and birds react to the presence of a predator by freezing, since motion is the surest way of attracting attention. Usually the prey stays still until it is clear that running is the only alternative, but occasionally one will hesitate a moment too long, and be captured by the snake. To a curious onlooker, it might appear that the snake 'charmed' its prey, but such is not the case.

Human snake charmers perpetuate a hoax on their audiences as well. The image of a 'charmed' cobra, swaying to the music of a flute, is as timeless as it is wrong; the snake, being deaf to airborne sound, is reacting to the movements of the charmer's body and instrument, matching sway for sway in order to keep the target in alignment should it decide to strike. The cobra may also be defanged, or have its mouth sewn shut, but in some regions of Asia newly caught king cobras are used in a dangerous ceremony that culminates with the charmer kissing the top of the rearing snake's head. The snakes are later released unharmed.

Snakes have figured in human mythology for millennia, only rarely cast in a good light. More often, from the Garden of Eden to the serpent-haired Medusa, snakes have been seen as an embodiment of evil. They have often been construed as messengers of the gods, benign or malicious depending upon the circumstances. In the US, while the Hopi Indians of the Southwest use snakes – especially rattlesnakes – in their famous snake dance to bring the rains, in the North-east the Iroquois and other woodland tribes feared to recount legends in the summer, when snakes would hear them and carry their stories to the gods.

CONSERVATION

◆◆◆◆◆◆◆◆◆◆◆◆◆◆◆

Sadly, to many people even today, the only good snake is a dead snake. Lacking big, soft eyes and an endearing face, snakes to not receive the attention the public lavishes on endangered birds or mammals, and yet there are many species of snakes in serious trouble around the world.

The reasons for this situation are varied, but the major causes are habitat destruction, uncontrolled killing (frequently for commercial purposes) and excessive collection for the pet trade. Some snakes, such as pythons, face all three pressures, and are rapidly losing ground in the wild. Indian pythons (*Python molurus*) are an excellent example: across Asia, their preferred habitat of grasslands and forest is rapidly being converted to pasture for livestock, with particular losses around permanent water sources, which the python requires; juveniles are collected in large num-

bers for the pet trade; while adults, which take years to mature, are slaughtered for the exotic leather industry, converted to boots, hat bands and belts.

The 1975 Convention of International Trade in Endangered Species (CITES) granted global protection to some snakes, although the treaty relies on the cooperation of both producer and importer nations, many of which are willing to look the other way for the sake of a lucrative business. The treaty has three levels of restriction, known as appendices. Appendix I lists those species threatened with immediate extinction, and prohibits their trade except for limited scientific and education uses. The Indian python is an Appendix I species, while the other pythons and boas are listed under Appendix II. This appendix includes plants and animals not immediately in danger of extinction, but

for which uncontrolled trade is likely to result in their becoming endangered. Some commercial trade in these species is permitted. Finally, Appendix III contains those animals and plants not listed In the first two appendices, but which are listed as threatened or endangered in certain countries. Appendix III protection has been invoked for a number of venomous snakes from Honduras, a severely deforested nation, including eyelash palm pit-vipers (*Bothriechis schlegelii*), jumping pit-vipers (*Porthidium nummifer*) and cantils (*Agkistrodon bilineatus*).

Unfortunately, it is relatively easy for countries to circumvent the CITES regulations – and trade rules do nothing to solve the larger problems of ignorant destruction and habitat loss. In most of the United States, snakes lack even the basic level of legal protection granted to birds, mammals or fish. A man who would be fined for catching a trout out of season can, in most areas, kill as many snakes as he wishes with impunity.

Protection for venomous species is unusual, and may only come when a species is on the brink of extinction – a point well illustrated in the United States. New York, which has only isolated populations of timber rattlesnakes, has declared them a threa-tened species and made killing them a crime. In neighbouring Pennsylvania, where rattlesnake populations are larger but still declining at an alarming rate, it is no crime to kill a rattlesnake, and organized rattlesnake hunts are still permitted. While the snakes now must be released after the hunt, the rough handling, display and disturbance is a serious problem.

The situation is even worse across the South and South-west, where giant rattlesnake hunts are a common form of civic fund-raising. Here, the rattlesnakes usually end up in the pot instead of back in the wild, and the participants still see the hunts as a way of reducing a dangerous and otherwise useless animal – over-looking the vital role snakes play in the balance of nature. Gasoline poured down burrows is a common way of flushing the snakes to the surface, with predictably bad effects.

Nevertheless, attitudes towards snakes are changing for the better, albeit slowly. The rise of the environmental movement has brought an increased awareness of the value of all living things, and a reappraisal of mankind's view of snakes. It can only be hoped that prejudice will be set aside in time to save those species already suffering badly at human hands.

LEFT
Jumbled boulders on dry mountainsides provide winter quarters for timber rattlesnakes *(Crotalus horridus)*, as well as an abundance of small mammals during the summer.

SNAKE FAMILIES

ABOVE
Rarely seen even by biologists, *Ungaliophis continentalis*
is a dwarf boa from Central America. Very little is known
about its life history or habits.

FAMILY

BOIDAE

(BOAS AND PYTHONS)

All five of the 'giant snakes', as well as some small to medium-sized species, belong to this ancient family of boas and pythons. They can be found in a wide range of habitats around the world, which would account for their diverse physical appearance. Their important attributes, anatomically speaking, are flexible jaws as well as a pelvic girdle and vestigial hind limbs. Moreover, it is likely that the left lung functions in addition to the right, a primitive characteristic found in only one other species: the sunbeam snake *(Xenopeltis unicolor)*.

SUBFAMILY

PYTHONINAE

While it is likely a boa (the anaconda) is the largest snake in the world, the pythons are, as a group, the giants among the serpents. There are 27 species of pythons found in Africa, Asia and Australia (with one in Central America), several of which have been known to reach more than 25 or 30ft (7.5 or 9m) in length.

Some of the world's most attractive snakes are pythons, with patterns that blend rich yellows, browns, russets, oranges and reds. Most pythons are solidly built, with long, lance-shaped heads and heavy bodies, although some of the arboreal species are much slimmer. The eyes, as with boas, feature vertical 'cat-eye' pupils, giving these huge snakes a distinctive look. The skull contains two bones missing in advanced families – the supra-orbitals in the top of the head, and the coronoid bone in the lower jaw. (Boas also possess the coronoid, which lends rigidity to the jaw.)

Pythons are egg-layers, and parental care – a rarity among reptiles – has been observed in many species, with the female curling around the eggs during much of the development stage. Female Indian pythons *(Python molurus)* may even undergo constant muscular spasms, which raise their body temperature and keep the eggs warm, if the air temperature drops below about 86°F (30°C). The twitching muscles may raise the python's body temperature as much as 13°F (7°C) above the ambient level. Some of the world's pythons:

RETICULATED PYTHON

◆◆◆◆◆◆◆

Python reticulatus

Found in South-east Asia and the Philippines, the reticulated python is one of the world's largest snakes, with lengths of more than 30ft (9m) accepted, and larger sizes claimed. As with all giant snakes, the true maximum size remains clouded in exaggeration and conjecture, but this is without doubt one of the planet's premiere reptiles.

Reticulated pythons are a cryptic mix of brown, buff and ochre, with a lovely, iridescent blue sheen on freshly moulted specimens. They feed largely on mammals, and exceptionally large pythons may ambush deer and pigs. There are occasional reports of reticulated pythons killing human beings.

INDIAN PYTHON
♦♦♦♦♦♦♦
P. molurus

At more than 20ft (6m), the Indian python is second only to the reticulated in size. There are at least three sub-species – one lighter in colour, native to India, a smaller Sri Lankan form, and *P. m. bivittatus,* the Burmese python, much darker and larger, found in South-east Asia and Indonesia. Many snake enthusiasts consider the Indian python the most beautiful of the group, with its crisp, somewhat angular markings of brown and yellow, and the Burmese is the most highly prized of all.

BALL PYTHON
♦♦♦♦♦♦♦
P. regius

Sometimes known as the royal python, this small species is found in Central and West Africa, where it inhabits dry forest, savanna and thorn scrub. Maximum size is about 6 or 7ft (1.8 or 2m) with the average about half that.

Ball pythons are so named for their characteristic de-fence posture, a tightly twined ball with the head inside. The background colour is dark brown, with lighter, irregu-larly rounded blotches providing good camouflage against the tawny undergrowth.

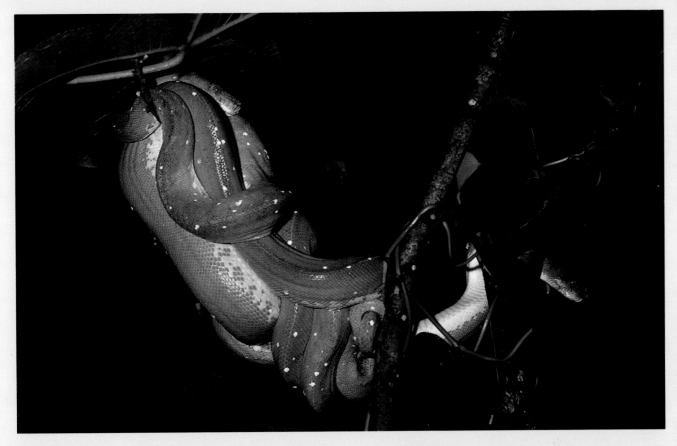

FACING PAGE
The Burmese python is a subspecies of the widespread Indian python *(Python molurus)*, and one of the largest and most attractive of this family of heavyweights.

ABOVE
Two green tree pythons *(Chondropython viridis)* curl about a branch – and each other – blending in well with the scenery. This species and the emerald tree boa *(Corallus canina)*, though not closely related and living half a world apart, have evolved in remarkably similar ways.

GREEN TREE-PYTHON

♦♦♦♦♦♦♦

Chondropython viridis

When two distantly related species develop in the same way in similar environments, the result is known as convergent evolution – and the green tree-python of Papua New Guinea and surrounding islands is an excellent example. Both it and the emerald tree boa (*Corallus canina*) of South America are arboreal constrictors that specialize in catching birds; both are lime green with yellow markings down the spine, and both have prehensile tails for a better grip on tree branches. The young of both are yellow or reddish, turning green with age. Both even rest in the same, unusual fashion, with coils looped over a narrow branch and the head lying in the middle on top. At first glance it is hard to believe they are not the same species.

Green tree-pythons are fairly small, with a maximum size of about 6ft (1.8m) – an adaptation to climbing, where large size is a disadvantage. In addition to birds, lizards and bats are also eaten.

ROCK PYTHON

♦♦♦♦♦♦♦

P. sebae

Another African species, the rock python reaches lengths of 20ft (6m), although some authorities credit reports of rock pythons of 32ft (9.75m).

A specialist in warm-blooded prey, rock pythons are noteworthy for their ability to eat antelope, gazelle and similar large mammals.

SUBFAMILY
BOINAE

ABOVE
The Mexican red-tailed boa is one of many subspecies of
the boa constrictor *(Boa constrictor)* found in Central and
South America.

Boas and pythons are frequently confused, since both groups are generally tropical, are constrictors and include a number of giant species. Both also retain vestigial hind limbs and other throwbacks to their lizard-like past. But there are significant differences, including the boa's lack of teeth on the premaxillary, lack of the supraorbital bone in the head and the presence of a single row of scales under the tail, rather than the paired scutes found in pythons. Boas are also live-bearers rather than egg-layers.

Boas are primarily a New World subfamily, with the greatest diversity of species in the Neotropics, and only a relative handful scattered over the western United States, Africa, southern Eurasia and the Indo-Pacific islands. In all there are about 40 species – more than the pythons, but with fewer monstrous species. The largest of all is the anaconda of South America, for which lengths of 37½ft (11.4m) have been claimed. If accurate (and the measurements of giant snakes are often educated guesswork rather than science), the anaconda would be the world's biggest snake, nudging out the slimmer reticulated python.

ABOVE
A close relative of the more famous emerald tree boa, the Amazon tree boa *(Corallus enydris)* may be yellow or brownish, while several subspecies have dark blotches or barring. It is found across most of northern South America.

BOA CONSTRICTOR

◆◆◆◆◆◆◆

Boa   constrictor

In the public mind, the jungle is a dangerous place, in part because of the fear of boa constrictors dropping on the unsuspecting passer-by, a scene played out in many bad adventure movies. In truth, boa constrictors are rather small (averaging about 6ft (1.8m), with a maximum of 18ft (5.5m)) and inoffensive, and while they may bite if provoked, they pose no threat to human beings. They are common throughout the Neotropics, as far north as Mexico and over much of South America to Argentina, in habitats that range from primary rainforest to savannas. Boa constrictors are excellent swimmers, and have been found on mangrove cayes well offshore of the Central American coast, where they feed predominantly on the eggs and young of nesting seabirds.

Boa constrictors have long been the most popular of the *Boidae* with pet-owners, since they tame quickly, breed well in captivity, and are very attractive. The head is long and somewhat boxy, with a dark postocular line extending to the rear of the jaw. Colour varies greatly with region and individuals, but most boa constrictors have a light background tone or buff, yellow or orange, overlaid with irregular dark blotches and crossbars that may have a lovely, reddish cast.

ANACONDA

◆◆◆◆◆◆◆

Eunectes   murinus

A true Goliath among snakes, a mature anaconda is a magnificent reptile – thick and muscular, perhaps 15 or 20ft (4.5 or 6m) long and weighing several hundred pounds, languid in its strength. Anacondas, especially younger specimens, are also very attractive, with a greenish-yellow background colour marked by a row of large, black spots down the spine, and yellow spots ringed with black along the sides. The face is plain except for a black-edged yellow postocular stripe.

Anacondas lead a semi-aquatic existence. They are not especially good swimmers, but haunt the edges of rivers and swamps, lying in wait for large prey like cayman, peccaries, young tapirs and capybara, the 120lb (54.5kg) giant

rodents of the South American river forests. An anaconda's diet also includes a large percentage of fish, as well as turtles and ducks. Few predators can afford to be choosy about what they eat.

Anacondas are found from the northern Amazon basin to Paraguay, with the largest subspecies found in the north-eastern part of its range.

RUBBER BOA
◆◆◆◆◆◆◆
Charina bottae

One of the two boas found north of the Mexican border, the rubber boa's range extends from Utah and Wyoming to southern British Columbia and central California, making it the most northerly of all the boas.

A fairly small snake, the rubber boa is heavily built for its size, plain brown with vertical pupils; the common name is apt, since it does feel like a fake, rubber snake when handled. An old name was the 'two-headed' snake – a reference to the blunt tail.

The rubber boa is something of an ecological generalist, able to adapt to open inhabitats as well as forest, and equally adept underground and in trees, where it hunts rodents, shrews and lizards. It spends a great deal of time hiding under fallen logs and loose bark.

ROSY BOA
◆◆◆◆◆◆◆
Lichanura trivirgata

The other native American boa, the rosy boa is seldom more than 3ft (1m) long. An attractive snake it has a background colour that ranges from rose to grey, marked with three irregular, lateral stripes.

The three subspecies of rosy boa have fairly restricted ranges in the United States, found in desert and scrubland in south-western Arizona and southern California. Rosy boas are often found near water, not because they require it (much of their liquid demands are met through their food) but because the birds and small mammals on which they feed are attracted to the water sources. Both rosy and rubber boas curl into tight balls when threatened, keeping their heads buried safely inside. Their blunt tails may be a way of luring predators into attacking the wrong end.

ABOVE
Highlights flicker across the prismatic scales of a Brazilian rainbow boa *(Epicrates c. cenchria)*, a species common in forests and near fields in South America.

FAMILY
LEPTOTYPHLOPIDAE

(THREAD SNAKES, SLENDER BLIND SNAKES)

At first glance, a slender blind snake may be mistaken for an earthworm, and indeed, one of their common names is 'worm snake', alluding to the pinkish colour and almost non-existent eyes.

Members of the *Leptotyphlopidae*, the slender blind snakes or thread snakes, inhabit a wide range that includes most of South and Central America, Mexico, the South-western United States, Africa, and the Middle East to Pakistan. They are burrowers that feed predominantly on insects and arthropods, and have such a primitive body structure — small scales, no belly scutes, a degenerate pelvic girdle and vestigial hind limbs — that they may be a close link to the lizard-like stock from which snakes arose. Some people have gone so far as to suggest that they be classified as legless lizards rather than true snakes.

In parts of South-west America, eastern screech-owls have discovered a novel use for Texas blind snakes (*Leptotyphlops dulcis*) — nest sanitation. The owls, which often eat small snakes, instead capture the blind snakes alive and carry them back to their nest holes, where they are released in the accumulated mat of old prey remains, droppings and food pellets. The blind snakes eat the larvae and pupae of such avian parasites as bot flies, providing a healthier environment for the owl chicks than would otherwise be the case.

LEFT
Almost sightless, and looking more like an earthworm than a snake, the western blind snake *(Leptotyphlops humilis)* is a burrower that feeds on insects and other tiny invertebrates.

FAMILY
ANOMALEPIDAE

(DAWN BLIND SNAKES)

This family of primitive snakes encompasses about 20 species, all found in Central and South America. Members of the genus *Anomalepis* resemble typical and slender blind snakes in general body shape and lifestyle, but have one or two teeth in the lower jaw, compared to none in typical blind snakes. They are burrowers, feeding on tiny invertebrates.

The *Anomalepidae* are sometimes classified with the typhlopids.

FAMILY
TYPHLOPIDAE

(TYPICAL BLIND SNAKES)

The largest family of blind snakes, with more than 160 species, the *Typhlopidae* are found in Central and South America, Africa, southern Eurasia from Greece to China, Indonesia and Australia. While not strictly tropical, they require a warm environment.

Typical blind snakes lack any teeth in the lower jaws, have tiny, nearly useless eyes, specialized rostral shields that form rounded or beaked snouts and even the remnants of a pelvis. The tail is usually blunt, and the body (especially in large species) may be quite robust.

One typhlopid, the Brahminy blind snake (*Typhlops braminus*), appears to be a consistently parthenogenetic species – that is, a completely female species that reproduces without fertilization from males. Known as the 'flowerpot snake', it is extremely common in parts of India, and has been introduced accidentally to Hawaii, imported in the roots of plants.

FAMILY

ANILIIDAE

(PIPESNAKES)

A primitive group, the pipesnakes retain a nonfunctional pelvis and vestigial hind limbs, but have a reduced left lung, suggesting that they are a bridge between even more primitive forms and the more advanced boas.

One species of pipesnake is found in the Amazon basin, with ten others in parts of South-east Asia. With their red and black banding, most effectively mimic local poisonous species, particularly coral snakes. One, the Malayan pipesnake (*Cylindrophus maculatus*), imitates not only the pattern but also the behaviour of a cobra, raising and waving its red-banded tail when disturbed, while hiding its head. The effect is of a venomous snake rearing for a strike.

Because pipesnakes have a fairly rigid, fused skull, they are unable to swallow very large items of food as more advanced snakes can. Instead, they concentrate on slender prey, especially other snakes and eels. Aniliids spend a large amount of their time underground, searching through burrows for prey.

FAMILY

TROPIDOPHIIDAE

(PROTOCOLUBROIDS)

The bulk of this obscure family is found in the West Indies, with three species found in Mexico and South America. Commonly known as woodsnakes, when disturbed they twine into a tight ball, head in the middle, while secreting a strong musk from the anus. This is not unusual, since many snakes have anal discharges that discourage predators. What borders on the bizarre is the woodsnake's ability to also bleed profusely from special blood vessels in the roof of the mouth, an act which presumably has some defensive value.

The two most interesting members of the *Tropidophiidae* are the Round Island 'boas', found only on Round Island in the Indian Ocean, near the island of Mauritius. While similar to true boas (with which they were classified for many years) *Bolyeria multocarinata* and *Casarea dussumieri* have no traces of hind limb bones, and the left lung is much smaller than in the primitive boas.

FAMILY
UROPELTIDAE

(SHIELDTAIL SNAKES)

About two dozen species of burrowing snakes from India and Sri Lanka make up the family *Uropeltidae,* the shieldtail snakes. Their common name comes from the strangely truncated shape of the tail exhibited by many species, which looks as though it had been sliced off at an angle and the diagonal cut shingled over with scales. The tail serves as an anchor, permitting the snake to push forwards through the soil.

The skull bones are fused more so than in advanced snakes, but unlike other blind snakes, the upper and lower jaws both have teeth. The eyes are minute and covered with a generalized scale, rather than a specialized brille, or eye spectacle. Shieldtails are often brightly patterned.

FAMILY
COLUBRIDAE

('TYPICAL' SNAKES)

The family *Colubridae* is the largest and most diverse group of snakes in the world, with more than 1,500 species. The vast majority are harmless, although research has shown that a surprising number have mildly venomous saliva, and one group, the opisthoglyphous colubrids, includes a number of rear-fanged species like the vine snakes, mussurana and blunt-headed tree snake that pose no true threat to human beings. Rear-fanged snakes lack an efficient envenomation system, and most have toxins specific to their prey; the genus *Fordonia* of Indonesia, for instance, has venom specific to crabs. One of the few exceptions is the African boomslang, whose venom is potent, and which can inject a lethal dose with a quick bite, rather than by chewing as in other colubrids.

In some ways, the colubrids are the intermediaries between the primitive snakes and the advanced, venomous members of the *Elapidae* and *Viperidae.* To view them simply as links, however, is to ignore the colubrids' tremendous success, since they make up more than half of all the world's snakes, and occupy every landmass except Antarctica.

SUBFAMILY
XENODONTINAE
I: Solid-toothed colubrids

Few snakes – indeed, few reptiles – have as wide a behavioural repertoire as the hognose snakes, a group restricted to the United States and Canada, and the best-known members of the subfamily *Xenodontinae*.

Robust and attractively patterned, hognose snakes (genus *Heterodon*) usually have dark blotches against a lighter brown or buff background. The name comes from the sharply upturned snout, which gives the snake a distinctive appearance. The head is flat and quite wide, frequently leading to misidentification as a venomous copperhead.

Hognoses are most often found in light, sandy soils, where they can burrow (with the use of their specialized snout) for toads, their primary food. Totally inoffensive, hognose snakes can rarely, if ever, be induced to bite – but they are not without defences. When disturbed, the snake launches into a disconcerting act, coiling and hissing with surprising volume, while puffing itself up and spreading a cobra-like hood; it may strike, but the mouth is usually closed. If that fails, the hognose will musk profusely, gaping its mouth wide to display its purple interior. If that doesn't scare off the intruder, the snake will begin to writhe as though in convulsions, smearing itself with musk. The performance ends with the snake lying limply on its back, mouth open and tongue out, to all appearances quite dead. Should it be rolled onto its stomach, the snake simply flips back over again.

There are four species of hognose snakes in North America – the eastern, southern, western and Mexican. The eastern is the richest in terms of coloration, with patches of russet mixed with the dark spots; there is also an all-black phase, a rare reddish phase and a small number of intermediary forms.

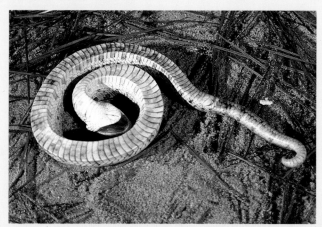

Hognose snakes (genus *Heterodon*) have a complicated bluff display that begins with a spread hood, gaping mouth and vigorous hissing, and ends with the snake on its back, feigning death.

SUBFAMILY

DASYPELTINAE

I: Solid-toothed colubrids

A number of snakes feed on bird eggs, but none have specialized in this diet to the degree achieved by the African egg-eating snake (*Dasypeltis scabra*), and related species.

Any snake is capable of swallowing prey larger than its head, but the egg-eating snakes can manage eggs an astonishing three times the head diameter – the rough equivalent of a person swallowing a large pumpkin whole. The snake is understandably methodical, first testing the egg with its tongue to avoid those that are rotten. (It also shies away from eggs with a well-developed embryo, although how it knows this from odour alone isn't clear.) The selection made, the snake throws a loose coil around the egg to hold it in place, then begins to ease its mouth around one end of the shell. The elasticity of the sides of the jaw and the neck skin beggars belief, as the egg is slowly 'walked' down the snake's throat.

A lump as massive as that caused by an egg would be a serious impediment, so the egg-eating snake has 25 or 30 modified vertebral spurs that jut into the throat. Once the egg is completely swallowed, the snake arches its neck, first puncturing and then collapsing the egg. The contents are forced down to the stomach, while the shell is regurgitated shortly after.

Egg-eating snakes average 2 or 3ft (0.6 or 1m) in length, and are yellowish-brown with dark patches. *D. scabra* is found in dry forests and brush throughout much of sub-Saharan Africa. In areas where birds breed seasonally, the egg-eating snake simply fasts once the nesting period ends.

SUBFAMILY
NATRICINAE
I: Solid-toothed colubrids

This subfamily contains some of the most familiar snakes in North America, the garter snakes and water snakes, common in backyards, along streams and can even be found in vacant city lots. They are live-bearers.

NORTHERN WATER SNAKE
♦♦♦♦♦♦♦
Nerodia sipedon,
formerly
Natrix sipedon

Aggressive but harmless, the northern water snake is nevertheless frequently mistaken for the venomous cottonmouth – even in areas hundreds of miles north of the cottonmouth's range.

Water snakes are rarely found far from water, where they lead a semi-aquatic lifestyle, basking on branches over-hanging the surface and diving for cover at the first hint of danger. If cornered they strike vigorously, and the bite from a 3ft (1m) water snake, while not toxic, is without doubt, very unpleasant.

Adult northern water snakes, especially those preparing to moult, may appear to be plain grey-brown. A freshly shed snake, a youngster or one that is wet will be much more colourful, with dark crossbands of brown or deep rust. The belly has an intricate pattern of reddish or brownish half-moons.

Northern water snakes are opportunistic feeders, but prey most often on fish, frogs, salamanders and toads.

ABOVE
Water snakes are rarely found far from water, and as soon as danger threatens they dive for cover beneath the surface. This is a midland water snake *(Nerodia sipedon pleuralis)*, a southern variety of the northern water snake.

LEFT
The vivid patterns of this juvenile northern water snake *(Nerodia sipedon)* will fade to obscurity as the snake matures.

COMMON GARTER SNAKE

◆◆◆◆◆◆◆

*Thamnophis sirtalis
and subspecies*

The most wide-ranging snake in North America, the
common garter snake is found from Nova Scotia to the
Gulf of Mexico, and from coastal California to the southern
edge of the North-west Territories. There are at least nine
subspecies, some found over huge swaths of land, while
others (like the endangered San Francisco garter snake)
are restricted to tiny areas.

Garter snakes are variable in colour and pattern, but
there are a few constants to help with identification. The
species is slim, with a narrow head and keeled scales; there
is almost always a light lateral line down the spine, and

usually two other light lateral lines on the sides, although
these may be broken into spots. Several subspecies show
large amounts of red on the sides.

Exceptionally adaptable to different habitats, garter
snakes occur in farmland, forest, mountains, prairies and
suburbs. They are fondest of riparian habitats, however,
and can be found most frequently near the margins of
creeks, swamps, marshes and lakes. Its prey include earthworms, small frogs and toads, salamanders, insects and fish,
and larger specimens, approaching the maximum size of 3
or 4ft (1 or 1.2m), may feed on small birds and mammals.
Its ground-hugging form allows it to move quickly and
silently through crevices, logs or tall grass.

Related, commonly encountered species include the
plains garter snake (*T. radix*) and the ribbon snake (*T. sauri-
tus*), which is extremely thin and long-tailed.

SUBFAMILY
COLUBRINAE

I: Solid-toothed colubrids

This largest of snake subfamilies includes between a quarter and half of the world's snakes, depending on which genera are included under its umbrella. The *Colubrinae* include some of the best-known snakes, such as the rat snakes of the genus *Elaphe,* the racers and the kingsnakes.

RAT SNAKES
♦♦♦♦♦♦
genus *Elaphe*

A wide-ranging genus, the *Elaphe* rat snakes are found over much of the Old and New World. Although considerably smaller than the boas, the rat snakes are adept constrictors, and their fondness for rodents is reflected in the group's common name, although a variety of other prey is also taken; the four-lined rat snake (*E. quatuorlineata*) of the north-eastern Mediterranean, for example, specializes in eating bird eggs. Rat snakes are talented climbers, able to crawl up even smooth-barked, limbless trees with no trouble. These elaphids show a strong preference for warm-blooded prey and eggs; young rat snakes are, by contrast, indiscriminate.

Rat snakes have long been popular with pet-owners for their beautiful coloration and generally gentle disposition. One of the loveliest of all is the corn snake (*E. guttata*) of the south-eastern United States, also known as the red rat snake. Its form is typical of the *Elaphe* – long and slim, shaped vaguely like a loaf of bread if seen in cross-section, with a rounded back and flat belly (this separating rat snakes from the racers, which are round in cross-section). The corn snake's colour varies greatly depending on the individual and habitat; the background tone may be yellowish, orange or grey, with vivid blotches of chestnut or red rimmed with black.

LEFT
Even in adulthood, a mature black rat snake *(Elaphe obsoleta)* shows a hint of the pattern it bore as a juvenile, especially if – as with this snake – it is swollen with air to make itself look more imposing.

FACING PAGE
The western green rat snake *(Elaphe triaspis intermedia)* is a tree-dwelling species of the Mexican mountains, just entering the United States in southern Arizona.

The black rat snake (*E. obsoleta*) inhabits a much wider range, from New England to the Gulf and the southern Plains. A large snake that may reach 8ft (2.4m) but averages 4 or 5ft (1.2 or 1.5m), the black rat begins life as a greyish juvenile boldly marked with dark blotches. As the snake ages, the pattern becomes lost in increasing amounts of black, until the adult is plain black, with only the faintest hint of cross-barring. The rat snake's throat and underside are plain white, but the belly is not completely black, as it is in the case of the similar black racer.

There are a number of geographic races of the black rat snake that are quite different in coloration. The yellow rat snake (*E. o. quadrivittata*) of the South-east coastal plain is yellowish or greenish, with four dark lateral stripes; those from the Everglades may be orangish or pinkish. The grey rat snake (*E. o. spiloides*) of the southern Mississippi basin resembles a juvenile black rat snake, with a grey background colour and darker blotches.

RACERS AND WHIPSNAKES
◆◆◆◆◆◆
genera *Coluber* and *Masticophis*

Racers and whipsnakes are found in much of the western hemisphere and parts of Europe, Africa and Asia. Agile and hyperactive when disturbed, these snakes are exceedingly long and slim; although they are only marginally faster than other snakes, their slim build and darting motions make them seem lightning-quick. They are not constrictors.

The black racer (*C. constrictor*) is found over most of the United States and south into Central America. Over its wide range this smooth, glossy snake may be gun-metal blue, jet black, greenish-grey or flecked with white spots. Black racers can reach 6ft (2m) in length. The European whip snake (*C. jugularis*), common over much of Eurasia, may exceed 10ft (3m), having reached full maturity.

Snakes of the genus *Masticophis* are thinner and longer still than racers. There are several species in the United States. The whipsnakes are marked with lateral stripes, while the coachwhip (*M. flagellum*) lacks stripes against the pink, buff or reddish body colour. The coachwhip's common and scientific names refer to the tail's resemblance to a plaited leather riding crop – an apt analogy when a captive coachwhip is lashing its tail from side to side, trying to escape.

INDIGO SNAKE
◆◆◆◆◆◆
Drymarchon corais

One of the largest non-poisonous snakes in North America, the indigo snake (*Drymarchon corais*) inhabits a limited range in Florida and the South-east, where habitat destruction and illegal collecting have reduced its numbers so greatly that it is listed as a federally endangered species.

Mature indigo snakes may grow to 8ft (2.4m) or more, as thick as a man's arm, but most are smaller, perhaps 5 to 6ft (1.5 to 1.8m). Indigos are gorgeous snakes, having lustrous, iridescent blue-black coloration with splashes of chestnut on the face and chin. Opportunistic hunters, indigo snakes will take small mammals, birds, amphibians and lizards, and their appetite for venomous snakes (somewhat overstated) has earned them goodwill for years. Sadly, they do not tolerate development well, and their partial reliance on the burrows of gopher tortoises – also threatened – adds to their problems.

BELOW
The eastern coachwhip *(Masticophis f. flagellum)* is a dramatically marked snake, named for the fancied resemblance of its tail to a braided leather whip.

KINGSNAKES

◆◆◆◆◆◆

genus *Lampropeltis*

A large genus, *Lampropeltis* includes such well-known species as the kingsnakes, scarlet kingsnakes and milk snakes. They are constrictors, and have a reputation for eating other snakes, and some possess varying degrees of immunity to hemotoxic venom. A few species may be confused with rat snakes, but differ from the *Elaphe* by having smooth, unkeeled scales and single, undivided anal plates.

Kingsnakes are found over the southern two-thirds of the United States and south through Mexico, Central and parts of South America. The most widespread species is the common kingsnake (*L. getulus*), or chain snake, so named for its black body colour and thin, creamy crossbands that form a chainlike pattern. There is tremendous variability among kingsnake populations, however, even within this one species, and individuals may be speckled, blotched or nearly black. A number of species, including the scarlet kingsnake (*L. doliata*) and the Sonora Mountain kingsnake (*L. pyromelana*) mimic the red, yellow and black bands of the venomous coral snake.

The milk snake (*L. triangulum*) is a fascinating example of mimicry. In the north-east United States, where coral snakes do not occur, milk snakes are greyish with rusty blotches, but in the south-east, Gulf region and Texas, where the coral snake is found, the milk snakes neatly mimic its bright warning colours to confuse and repel potential predators.

RING-NECK SNAKE

◆◆◆◆◆◆

Diadophis punctatus

Among the most innocuous of snakes, the tiny ring-neck snake is a hunter of bugs and salamanders, spiders and worms, living in the damp world beneath rotting logs and between moss-grown rocks. As with many wide-ranging snakes, colour varies with locale. Those in the eastern United States and southern Canada are shiny black above and yellow or orange below; a thin band of the same colour encircles the neck. Western subspecies may be olive, blue-grey or black, and may lack the neck ring. Ring-neck snakes have been discovered from Nova Scotia to Florida and central Mexico, with a scattered distribution along the Pacific Coast and Great Basin.

FAMILY
COLUBRIDAE

II: Rear-fanged colubrids

The family *Colubridae* includes a small number of rear-fanged species, which come from the subfamilies *Colubrinae* and *Natricinae*. As already noted (page 101), most of the rear-fanged snakes are harmless to human beings, although prudence is always called for, since sensitivity to toxins may vary from person to person. Any large, rear-fanged snake should be treated with the same caution as an elapid or viper.

ABOVE
A Mexican species that barely crosses the border into Texas, the cat-eyed snake *(Leptodeira septentrionalis)* is a nocturnal, rear-fanged hunter of frogs.

LEFT
Known as the 'false water cobra', the Brazilian smooth snake *(Cyclagras gigas)* combines both constriction and rear-fanged venom in its hunting. In the wild, this large species is no threat to human beings.

FACING PAGE
The vine snake *(Oxybelis aeneus)* is sometimes feared because it is thought to be venomous, in part because it has a startling threat display in which it gapes its black mouth at intruders. Although it is a rear-fanged species, it is harmless to human beings.

MEXICAN VINE SNAKE

◆◆◆◆◆◆◆

Oxybelis aeneus

An almost alarming slim snake, the vine snake looks like a twig come to life – an understandable adaptation for life in the trees, both as an aid to climbing, and as camouflage from prey and predator alike. Vine snakes feed mostly upon lizards, especially anoles, which react quickly to the snake's venom. Mexican vine snakes normally reach a length of 5ft (1.5m), and are brown above and cream-yellow below. The head is long and the snout is extremely tapered.

FLYING SNAKES

◆◆◆◆◆◆◆

Chrysolopea

Of all the modes of snake locomotion, none is more re-markable than that of the five species of flying snakes, native to the rainforests of southern Asia. Rather than labouriously climbing down one tree and up the next, the flying snake simply lunges off into the void – and glides. Airborne, the snake assumes a stiff S-shape, while expand its somewhat elongated ribs so that the underside of the body becomes a wide, concave surface. The snake cannot glide as far, or as gracefully, as flying squirrels or flying lizards, but it can control its direction to a significant degree.

Flying snakes, also known as golden tree-snakes, are small, slim and large-headed, and feed on lizards, frogs, small birds and arboreal mammals.

BOOMSLANG

◆◆◆◆◆◆◆

Dispholidus typus

The most dangerous of the rear-fanged snakes, the boomslang is a common tree snake over most of sub-Saharan Africa. It comes in a confusing array of colours and patterns, from solid green to black, spotted, barred and almost everything in between. The pattern may be especially bold on the neck, which is inflated during threat displays.

Boomslangs are large (up to 5ft/1.5m), very fast, easily irritated and able to open their mouths to a greater degree than most colubrids, so that the fangs at the back of the mouth puncture the skin directly, without chewing. Even

worse, the boomslang's venom is potently hemotoxic and produced in large quantities, and there have been many human deaths. Another rear-fanged African snake, the twig snake, or bird snake (*Thelotornis kirtlandii*), has also been known to cause human fatalities.

FAMILY
ELAPIDAE

The elapids are universally venomous snakes, found in the middle latitudes around the world, and include such famous species as the king and monocled cobras, coral snakes and mambas. Two highly specialized subfamilies, the sea snakes of the *Hydrophiinae* and *Laticaudinae,* are the only truly pelagic snakes in the world.

Elapids have short, fixed fangs at the front of the mouth, a step of complexity above the rear-fanged snakes, but much simpler in design than the folding fangs of the vipers. Elapid venom varies widely, but tends to affect the nervous system rather than cause massive tissue damage.

All the venomous snakes of Australia are elapids, and they make up roughly 60 per cent of the continent's snake species, making this the only place in the world where poisonous snakes outnumber non-poisonous species.

Amongst the best-known of the Australian elapids are the black snake *Pseudechis porphyriacus*), found in swamps and woodlands in eastern and southern Australia. Averaging 4 to 6ft (1.2 to 1.8m), the black snake is glossy blue-black above and varying shades of red or orange below. When threatened it rears and spreads its neck. A common species with a strongly hemotoxic venom, the black snake accounts for most of the snake bites in Australia, but rarely causes death.

More serious are the bites of the tiger snake (*Notechis scutatus*), Australian brown snake (*Pseudonaja textilis*) and taipan (*Oxyuranus scutellatus*). The latter which reaches a length of 11ft (3.3m) has traditionally been considered one of the most dangerous snakes in the world.

SUBFAMILY
ELAPINAE

KING COBRA
◆◆◆◆◆◆◆
Ophiophagus hannah

The king cobra is the unchallenged monarch of venomous snakes – the largest species in the world, with specimens of more than 18ft (5.5m), and claims of records exceeding 20ft (6.1m). A king cobra of this size, rearing back, would almost be eye-to-eye with a human being.

For all its size, and the undisputed toxicity of its venom, the king cobra causes fewer fatalities than other venomous species in its range. The reasons are several: the king cobra is uncommon, it is shy and retiring, and it prefers undeveloped areas, rather than villages and rice patties haunted by the more dangerous monocled cobra.

King cobras are reptile-eaters, and specialize for hunting snakes and, to a lesser extent, lizards, through thick brush, bamboo stands and trees. The king cobra's pattern varies by region, from olive in Thailand to brownish in China. The hood is narrow, often with a dark band across the light throat patch.

The king cobra is found from China to India, and through the Philippine archipelago. It is the only snake known to build a nest, an elaborate, two-chambered mass of vegetation over which the female stands guard during the development period. Warmth for the eggs is provided by the heat of the decomposing plant matter.

MONOCLED COBRA
◆◆◆◆◆◆◆
Naja naja

Also known as the Indian or Asian cobra, this is the snake most people think of when the word 'cobra' is mentioned, with its wide, dramatic hood, marked on the back with one or two pale 'eye-spots' rimmed in black, a horseshoe, or bands; on dark individuals the hood may be absent. The snake itself may be as much as 5 or 6ft (1.5 or 1.8m) in length, with body coloration ranging from all black or brown to spotted or banded with white.

The hood of a cobra is nothing more than a skin flap, extended by elongated ribs when the cobra is startled or angry. At other times, the skin rests flat against the body, and the cobra looks much like any other snake.

Monocled cobras are found from China and Indonesia to the Caspian Mountains.

LEFT
The markings on the hood of the monocled cobra *(Naja naja)* vary quite a bit, from a spectacle mark to the simple ocellation seen here.

SPITTING COBRAS
♦♦♦♦♦♦♦
genera Naja, Hemachatus

Although monocled cobras will occasionally 'spit' venom, several African species have raised this form of self-defence to its highest expression. Lacking lips, the cobras do not really spit – instead they spray their venom by exhaling sharply while forcing the liquid from the venom glands through specially adapted fangs, which open to the front, rather than the rear. Spitting cobras aim for the eyes, and are accurate at ranges of 6 or 8ft (1.8 or 2.4m). If the shot hits the victim's eyes, nasal tissue or mouth, it causes burning pain and temporary blindness.

Biologists theorize that 'spitting' arose for the same reason that rattlesnakes evolved their rattles, as a method of steering away herds of large mammals that might trample the snake to death. The most widespread of this group is the black-necked cobra (*N. nigricollis*), with many distinctly marked subspecies. The ringhals (*H. haemachatus*) is restricted to southern Africa.

BANDED KRAIT
♦♦♦♦♦♦♦
Bungarus fasciatus

Kraits are medium-sized, nocturnal elapids found in southern Asia and Indonesia. Although highly venomous, they are fairly inoffensive, although in the past many people have been bitten when they rolled over in their sleep and startled a krait searching the hut for rodents, lizards or other snakes. The banded krait is yellow with dark crossbands, and has a peculiar, raised dorsal ridge. It is found from Borneo to southern India.

MAMBAS
♦♦♦♦♦♦♦
genus Dendroaspis

The mamba is perhaps the most feared snake in Africa, accused of unprovoked attacks on humans. Of course, what passes for 'unprovoked' from a human perspective might not seem so to the snake, and in any event modern naturalists have found that the mambas, while undoubtedly deadly, do not live up to their reputation for ferocity.

Mambas are exceptionally quick, and when cornered will bite with speed and accuracy. They are long – averaging 6 to 10ft (1.8 to 3m), with records of 14ft (4.2m) mambas – and very slim. The green mambas, of which there are several species, are arboreal, while the black mamba (*D. polylepis*) spends a great deal more time on the ground. The western green mamba (*D. viridis*) is arrestingly marked, with very large, bright green scales against darker skin. The head is long and narrow. Green mambas are usually considered less aggressive than black mambas.

CORAL SNAKES
◆◆◆◆◆◆

genera *Micruroides*, *Micrurus*, *Leptomicrurus*

Brightly banded to warn off predators, the coral snakes back up their threat with a poweful neurotoxin. Conse-quently, many tropical snake-eating birds, like motmots and large flycatchers, have learned to avoid snakes with bands of yellow and red.

There are more than 50 species of true coral snakes in the New World, unrelated to the venomous coral snakes of Asia. There are two species that occur in the United States – the eastern coral snake (*Micrurus fulvius*), on the coastal plain from South Carolina to south Texas, and the Arizona coral snake (*Micruroides euryxanthus*), in southern Arizona and south-west New Mexico. Secretive and un-aggressive, they rarely bite, although tropical species, which are larger, may be less tolerant of human beings. All should be considered highly dangerous.

HYDROPHIINAE and LATICAUDINAE

(SEA SNAKES)

While many snakes exploit the rich resources found at the water's edge, only these two subfamilies have made the evolutionary leap to a pelagic lifestyle, and only one has severed all connection with land. Of the two groups, the *Laticaudinae* are the less specialized, spending much of their time on land where they lay their eggs. The *Hydro-phiinae*, on the other hand, are true creatures of the sea, never coming ashore, and bearing live young in the water. They are, of course, still air-breathers, but are capable of staying submerged for long periods of time. Their tails are dorsally compressed for better propulsion, the nostrils are equipped with closure flaps and are set high on the head for surface breathing. Like many oceanic birds, sea snakes also possess head glands that rid the body of excess salt.

Little is known about sea snakes, even though by some estimates they are the most common snakes in the world. Most are warm-water animals, found from the Red Sea to New Zealand and Japan. One genus is also found along parts of east Africa and the Pacific coast of Central and South America, but none occur in the Atlantic.

Sea snakes produce some of the most toxic venoms known, and during the breeding season can be extremely aggressive, although most bites are suffered by commercial fishers who inadvertently catch the snakes in their nets.

FAMILY
VIPERIDAE

(VIPERS)

The vipers represent the pinnacle of venomous evolution among snakes. Even those with an irrational fear of snakes must admire the efficiency of viperine system, which depends on a pair of long, hinged fangs that fold flat against the roof of the mouth when not needed, but can flip forward and lock into place when the jaws swing open.

There are three subfamilies. One, the *Azemiopinae*, has but a single member, Fea's viper *(Azemiops feae)* of southern China and neighbouring regions. The Old World vipers of the *Viperinae* are considered somewhat more primitive than the *Crotalinae*, or pit vipers, which possess thermoreceptive pits between the eye and nostril that help them locate prey.

ABOVE
Found in various forms and subspecies from the
Mediterranean to Afghanistan and the Soviet Union, the
Levant viper *(Vipera lebetina)* is one of the few snakes
that can both lay eggs or bear live young. It is a leading
cause of snakebite fatalities within its range.

VIPERINAE

The *Viperinae* are restricted to the Old World, and include some of the planet's most dangerous snakes, including the saw-scaled viper and the puff adder. Although Shakespeare credits Cleopatra's suicide to an asp (perhaps the horned desert viper, *Cerastes cerastes*), modern scholars think a cobra, revered in Egypt and providing a relatively easy death, would be a more logical choice than the violently painful venom of a viper.

GABOON VIPER
◆◆◆◆◆◆◆
Bitis gabonica

The Gaboon viper, a heavyweight among its peers, may grow to as much as 7ft (2.1m), and has fangs to match its girth – more than 2in (5cm) from base to tip, the longest fangs of any snake. Sheer mass makes the Gaboon viper an awe-inspiring snake, but it is usually lethargic and slow to take offence, apparently relying more on its excellent forest-floor camouflage than on venom for protection. While few deaths from Gaboon viper bites are reported, the quantity of venom it is capable of injecting makes it a potentially very dangerous snake.

Gaboon vipers are found in rainforests across central Africa, where they ambush birds and mammals, occasionally taking prey as large as small antelope.

ABOVE
A Gaboon viper *(Bitis gabonica)* is coloured to match to the pattern of fallen leaves in the African forest, where this massive viper is found.

PUFF ADDER
◆◆◆◆◆◆◆
B. arietans

Highly feared, the puff adder is a leading cause of snakebite in sub-Saharan Africa, although the mortality rate from this species is probably lower than from the saw-scaled viper.

Puff adders are large and heavily built, averaging 3 or 4ft (1 or 1.2m) in length. Coloration is a cryptic mix of buff, brown and black, with alternating light and dark chevrons down the back. The powerful venom of the puff adder is said to have been used in a bizarre form of hunting; large snakes were caught and tied along game trails, bringing down animals as big as Cape buffalo.

LEFT
Living up to its name, a puff adder *(Bitis arietans)* swells up like a long balloon when angry.

SAW-SCALED VIPER

✦✦✦✦✦✦✦

Echis carinatus

Also known as the carpet viper, this small desert-dwelling species is considered the most dangerous snake over its wide range, from India through the Middle East to East Africa. In some regions, mortality from saw-scaled viper bites has exceeded 80 per cent, and lethal bites may be inflicted by specimens less than 12in (30cm) long. The venom is powerfully hemotoxic, causing massive bleeding and severe pain.

Saw-scaled vipers are named for the serrated scales on the lower flanks, which are dragged past each other as the snake writhes through its figure-8 threat display. The scales make a loud rasping sound, which is accentuated by the snake's hissing.

EUROPEAN ADDER

✦✦✦✦✦✦✦

Vipera berus

The only venomous snake in Great Britain and northern Europe, the adder has an exceedingly wide range, spanning Europe and Asia as far as Korea. It is the only snake found north of the Arctic Circle, withstanding the cold of the Soviet winter.

Adders are small, rarely longer than 2ft (0.6m), with the record just under 3ft (1m). Background colour varies from grey and olive to yellow or brown, with a dark zigzag line running down the back, and a 'V' or 'X' mark on the head. Because of its small size and rather placid disposition, the European adder rarely causes human fatalities.

RUSSELL'S VIPER

✦✦✦✦✦✦✦

V. russellii

One of the most attractive true vipers, Russell's viper is usually brownish-yellow or grey, with a series of linked, brown ovals, rimmed in black and white, running down the spine, and smaller rimmed spots along the sides. This species is common from Pakistan to China and south through parts of Indonesia, most often found in brush and along the edges of fields, which accounts for the extremely high incidence of snakebites attributed to it.

LEFT
The zigzagging back stripe and dark postocular line are characteristic of the Ottoman, or Near East, viper *(Viper xanthina)*, found from Turkey to Israel and Iran. While it accounts for many snakebites annually, the fatality rate is low.

CROTALINAE

The *Crotalinae* is primarily a New World subfamily, reaching its greatest diversity in the south-western deserts (among rattlesnakes) and the Neotropics (the various palm and related vipers, many formerly in the genus *Bothrops*). There are also a number of tree vipers, *Agkistrodon* moccasins and other pit vipers which inhabit Asia.

The distinctive mark of the *Crotalinae* are their heat-sensing facial pits, located between the nostril and eye. The pits provide the snake with a highly accurate targeting system for hunting small, warm-blooded prey in the dark.

COTTONMOUTH

◆◆◆◆◆◆◆

Agkistrodon piscivorous

Perhaps better known as the 'water moccasin', the cottonmouth is a semi-aquatic pit viper common in the southern United States lowlands, from southern Virginia to central Texas, and north in the Mississippi basin to Illinois. Stout-bodied snakes, cottonmouths have light and dark crossbarring against a dusky background, with a light face and pronounced postocular line. Western specimens tend to be all dark, with little or no facial pattern. Pugnacious, a cottonmouth will frequently stand its ground when harassed, often, as a warning signal, opening its mouth to display the white linings that give it its name.

The cantil (*A. bilineatus*) of Mexico is similar in shape, dark brown with thin, light crossbars and a wide postocular line that covers most of the cheek. An Asian representative, the mamushi (*A. blomhoffi*) of Japan and Korea, accounts for few fatalities, while the sharp-nosed viper, or 'hundred pacer' (*Deinagkistrodon acutus*, formerly *A. acutus*) of China, Vietnam and Taiwan, is one of the most dangerous of Asian snakes.

ABOVE
There is no mistaking the menace in the gaping display of a cottonmouth. Note that even though the mouth is open, the fangs have not been swung forward into the striking position.

LEFT
The western subspecies of the cottonmouth (*Agkistrodon piscivorous leucostoma*) shares with its eastern cousin a far more potent venom than that of their American relation – the copperhead.

BELOW
In Mexico and Central America, the cottonmouth is
replaced by the very similar cantil *(Agkistrodon
bilineatus)*. This is a young Taylor's cantil, which still bears
the yellow tail of a juvenile. Baby copperheads and
cottonmouths also have yellow tail tips, which may serve
as a lure for frogs and toads.

COPPERHEAD

♦♦♦♦♦♦♦

A. contortrix

Possibly the least offensive venomous snake in North America, the copperhead has a placid personality and a relatively weak venom. Bites are uncommon even where this species is fairly abundant, and fatalities are almost unheard of. Only children are at serious risk from a copperhead bite.

Copperheads are attractive snakes, blending rusty browns, pinks, oranges or yellows in a series of dark hourglass marks against a lighter background. The head is un-marked, with a brighter line of yellow or orange around the mouth; the belly is plain, except for dark spots along the edges. A snake of uplands, the copperhead is often found in the same habitat as timber rattlesnakes, and may share the same hibernacula, usually deep crevices between boulders. Copperhead young are born in sacs, the last relic of an egg. Once free from these sheaths (roughly half an hour), the 9-inch snakes are already poisonous enough to kill small prey.

There are several subspecies. The northern copperhead is the duskiest, while the southern is much paler. Copperheads are found from southern New England to southeastern Nebraska, south to Florida and central Texas.

EYELASH PALM-PITVIPER

♦♦♦♦♦♦♦

Bothriechis schlegelii, formerly *Bothrops schlegelii*

The Neotropics are rich in small, arboreal pit vipers, many of them strikingly beautiful. The eyelash palm-pitviper is one of the prettiest – and most variable – of them all. Specimens may be glowing yellow, burnished gold, orangish, green, purplish, bluish, heavily flecked with brown, or speckled with a combination of almost all of the above. Regardless of colour, they may be identified by the jagged supraorbitals, which form the scaly 'eyelash'.

Eyelash palm-pitvipers spend almost all of their time above ground, waiting in the thick foliages of rainforest trees and shrubs. They are short and slim, with a strongly prehensile tail, adapted to hunting small rodents, lizards and frogs. They have developed another adaptation to life in the trees in that when they strike at prey they hold fast rather than let go, as do most pit vipers. The reason is that otherwise their meal would likely drop out of the tree, falling as much as 150ft (45.5m) to the ground.

LEFT
Also known as the purple-spotted pit viper, the mangrove pit viper *(Trimeresurus purpureomaculatus)* of Asia has several 'morphs', or colour phases, including this pale purple, spotless form.

ABOVE
By far the most variable of the pit vipers in the New World tropics, the arboreal eyelash palm-pitviper *(Bothriechis schlegelii)* comes in a confusing array of colours, including yellow, green, orange and purple.

BELOW
The yellow-lined palm viper *(Bothriechis lateralis)* is found in the jungles of Central America, living in the understorey and canopy of the forest.

FER-DE-LANCE

♦♦♦♦♦♦♦

Bothrops asper,
formerly B. atrox

Each continent has one venomous snake that is feared above all others. In Central and South America, it is the fer-de-lance, which causes more fatalities than any other species. There are a confusing number of local names, including yellow-jaw, yellow-tail, terciopelo, barba amarilla and tommigoff. A large pit viper, the fer-de-lance may grow to 8ft (2.4m), although the bite of far smaller specimens can be fatal. Death is accompanied by extensive bleeding, also a feature of bushmaster envenomation.

Fer-de-lances are cryptically patterned to blend with the forest floor, where they spend most of their time. The background colour is a variable shade of light brown, with dark arrowhead markings forming offset pairs down the spine. There is a dark and light postocular line on each side of the head.

BUSHMASTER

♦♦♦♦♦♦♦

Lachesis muta

The longest venomous snake in the New World, the bushmaster has been recorded at lengths of 12ft (3.6m), although 7 or 8ft (2.1 or 2.4m) is the normal maximum. Despite its size and massive venom yield, the bushmaster is responsible for relatively few human deaths each year. There is a corollary between it and the king cobra – both are large and greatly feared, but are rarely seen (the bushmaster is nocturnal) and prefer undisturbed forest away from human development. The bushmaster is found from Central America to the Amazon basin.

Bushmasters are heavy-bodied, with large, powerful-looking heads. The background colour is brownish, yellowish or reddish, with inverted dark triangles along the spine. There is a single dark postocular line running back from just behind the eye.

The rattlesnake is, with the cobra, the most unmistakable snake in the world. Virtually everyone recognizes the loosely joined, horny tail segments, which give the rattlesnake its name and a relatively effective warning system – if it chooses to use it. By no means do rattlesnakes always rattle, and some species habitually do not. There are roughly 30 species, with most found in the south-west United States and Mexico. One species, the timber rattlesnake *(C. horridus)*, is found as far north-east as southern New England, and another, the neotropical rattlesnake or cascabel *(C. durissus)*, occupies a wide range from Mexico to Argentina.

Representative among the rattlesnakes are:

TIMBER RATTLESNAKE

♦♦♦♦♦♦♦

Crotalus horridus

While most rattlesnakes have adapted to arid or desert conditions, the timber rattler has filled a niche in the US in the lush, humid forests of the east and south, living on rocky slopes and wooded valleys. There are two common colour phases – yellow or tan background tone with dark crossbars or blotches, and 'black phase', usually very dusky with just a hint of patterning. The phases are unrelated to age or sex. Freshly moulted specimens, particularly the yellow phase, have a lustrous, almost velvety appearance to their skin.

Timber rattlesnakes reach an average size of 3 or 4ft (1 or 1.2m), and a record maximum of 6ft (2m). They are rodent ambushers, waiting – at times for days – along runways used by mice and chipmunks. The canebreak rattlesnake *(C. h. atricaudatus)* is a subspecies of the timber rattler found from Texas to southern Virginia. It prefers lower, wetter habitats than the timber rattler, and has a dark postocular line on the head.

ABOVE RIGHT
The Arizona ridge-nosed rattlesnake *(Crotalus w. willardi)* only lives in two isolated mountain ranges on the Arizona-Mexico border.

RIGHT
A large, yellow-phase timber rattlesnake *(Crotalus horridus)* rests among the leaves of a New York State refuge set aside for this species, which is threatened with extinction in the State.

FACING PAGE, RIGHT
Found in Mexico and parts of the south-west United States, the Mojave rattlesnake *(Crotalus scutulatus)* possesses one of the most dangerous crotalid venoms, with powerful neurotoxic effects.

FACING PAGE, BOTTOM
By far the most adaptable of the American rattlesnakes, the western rattlesnake *(Crotalus viridis)* is found on prairies, along streams and even in mountain meadows. This is the prairie rattler *(C. v. viridis)*, one of the most common subspecies.

EASTERN DIAMONDBACK RATTLESNAKE
♦♦♦♦♦♦♦
C. adamanteus

The eastern diamondback is the largest venomous snake in North America, reaching lengths of 8ft (2.4m) or more. An inhabitant of pine flatwoods and saw palmetto thickets, it is found on the coastal plain which stretches from Louisiana to North Carolina.

The face is starkly marked with dark and white lines, and the diamonds along the spine are edged with black and cream. The eastern diamondback is a dangerous snake, if only for its size and tolerance of lightly developed areas, such as wooded neighbourhoods. They should, of course, be treated with great caution.

WESTERN DIAMONDBACK RATTLESNAKE
♦♦♦♦♦♦♦
C. atrox

An angry western diamondback is an imposing reptile. While not as big as the eastern diamondback – maximum size is 6ft (2m), the western has a dramatic threat display, in which the head and neck are raised high above the ground in the tight S-curve, while the black-and-white banded tail is prominently displayed.

Western diamondbacks are not as clearly marked as the eastern species, and background colour varies from grey or buff to brown and even reddish; the markings are indistinct. It is found from Texas and Oklahoma to southern California and south through Mexico.

SIDEWINDER
◆◆◆◆◆◆◆
C. cerastes

Any snake, trying to move through loose sand, will 'side-wind' – that is, throw out S-shaped loops in the direction of travel, thus anchoring itself while drawing the rest of the body along behind. But the sidewinder rattlesnake of the American south-west has achieved a degree of notoriety for this manoeuvre, common among desert snakes the world over.

Sidewinders are also known as 'horned rattlesnakes' for their pointed supraocular scales. The background colour is pale buff or grey, with small dark blotches or spots. A relatively small snake, sidewinders are usually less than 2ft (0.6m) long, and feed largely on nocturnal rodents.

PYGMY RATTLESNAKE
◆◆◆◆◆◆◆
Sistrurus miliarius

The smallest of the rattlesnakes, the pygmy rarely exceeds 20in (50cm) in length, and has a rattle that is more likely to be mistaken for a buzzing cricket than a snake's warning. Several subspecies are found across the south United States, from Texas and Florida to the Carolinas and southern Missouri. Eastern subspecies tend to be dark and heavily flecked, while western specimens are usually lighter, with distinct markings. A closely related species, the massasauga (S. catenatus), is found from western Pennsylvania, through the Midwest to Mexico, often in wet, low-lying areas. Pygmy rattlesnakes have nine large plates covering the tops of their heads instead of numerous small scales.

NEOTROPICAL RATTLESNAKE
◆◆◆◆◆◆◆
C. durissus

Also known as the cascabel, the neotropical rattlesnake inhabits dry terrain and farmland from the Gulf coast of Mexico through Central and South America. Stoutly built and cloaked in large scales, the cascabel has a distinct diamond pattern on the back, and two dark stripes that begin behind the eyes and run for several inches down the neck. The venom is strong and, in part, neurotoxic due to chemical crotamine, producing a 'broken neck' effect in victims.

GLOSSARY

◆◆◆◆◆◆◆◆◆◆◆◆◆◆

Aglyphous – Solid-toothed.

Anal plate – Large scute covering the snake's anus or vent; may be single or divided.

Antivenin – Serum made from the blood of horses (or other mammals) immunized against snake venom; used to treat human snakebite.

Arboreal – Living in trees.

Batesian mimicry – The imitation by a harmless or palatable species of a dangerous or unpalatable form.

Birthing rookery – Area where gravid (pregnant) female snakes gather to give birth.

Brille – Transparent scale covering the snake's eye.

Chorioallantois – Thin membrane layer in shelled eggs that permits transfer of gases.

Cloaca – Combined genital and anal opening in amphibians, reptiles and birds.

Colubrid – Member of the family *Colubridae*.

Constriction – Suffocating prey by wrapping it tightly in coils.

Convergent evolution – Evolution of two unrelated species into similar forms, in response to similar environmental pressures.

Coronoid – Bone in lower jaw, present in pythons and boas.

Duvernoy's gland – Specialized salivary gland in colubrids that produces venom.

Ecological niche – The position a living thing occupies within a natural community.

Ectothermy – Reliance upon external conditions to determine body temperature; cold-bloodedness'.

Egg tooth – A small, true tooth protruding from the mouth of snake hatchlings, used to slit open the egg shell.

Elapid – Member of the family *Elapidae*.

Endothermy – Possession of internal mechanisms to maintain an even body temperature, regardless of external conditions; 'warm-bloodedness'.

Envenomation – Injection of venom.

Estivation – Torpor brought on in response to extreme heat or drought; similar to hibernation.

Genera – Plural of genus.

Glottis – In snakes, the tubular opening to the windpipe.

Gravid – Carrying undelivered eggs or young; pregnant.

Hemotoxic – Toxin (venom) that attacks tissue.

Hibernacula – Dens in which animals hibernate (singular: hibernaculum).

Hibernation – Profound torpor featuring drastically reduced heartbeat, respiration and metabolism.

Immunity – Insusceptibility (to a toxin). Immunity may be inherent or induced.

Jacobson's organ – Nerve-rich pits in the roof of a snake's mouth, into which the tongue places odour particles; part of olfactory system.

Keel – Lengthwise ridge (scales)

Labial – Lip (scales).

Mental – Scale at tip of lower lip.

Müllerian mimicry – Convergence of colour or pattern among two or more dangerous or unpalatable species, thus reinforcing their mutual protection.

Musk – General term for defensive fluid discharged by paired glands adjoining anus in snakes.

Neurotoxic – Toxin (venom) that attacks nervous system.

Opisthoglyphous – Rear-fanged.

Oviparous – Egg-laying.

Parthenogenetic – Mode of reproduction in which eggs develop into offspring without fertilization by a male.

Postocular – Behind the eye (often a line or marking).

Prehensile – Adapted for grasping (tail).

Premaxillary – Bones at the front of the upper jaw.

Proteroglyphous – Possessing fixed, immobile fangs.

Rostral – Scale at the tip of the upper jaw.

Scute – Scale.

Sidewind – Complex movement by snake on loose sand, in which loops of the body are thrown forward to draw the snake across the ground.

Solenoglyphous – Possessing hinged, movable fangs.

Spp. – Plural abbreviation for species.

Supraocular – Above the eye (scales).

Supraorbital – Bone above eyes, present in pythons.

Thermoreceptive – Sensitive to heat (facial pits on pit vipers, boas, pythons).

Vent – Cloacal opening.

Vestigial – A degenerate or useless body part.

Viviparous – Live-bearing.

INDEX

◆◆◆◆◆◆◆◆◆◆◆◆◆◆

PICTURE CREDITS

◆◆◆◆◆◆◆◆◆◆◆◆◆◆